Wesley
Education

Self-Esteem:
A Family Affair

Leader Guide

West
Education

Self-Esteem: A Family Affair

Leader Guide

by Jean Illsley Clarke

Winston Press

Library of Congress Catalog Card Number: 80-53554
ISBN: 0-86683-976-3 (previously ISBN: 0-03-059064-7)
Printed in the United States of America

Winston Press, Inc.
430 Oak Grove
Minneapolis, MN 55403

5 4 3 2

PREFACE

These meeting plans were designed by Jean Illsley Clarke to honor people and to invite them to grow. The plans were tested and adjusted over a four year period by forty facilitators and over six hundred people in rural, urban, and suburban communities.

The Letters to Marj contain the collected wisdom of the people who have already facilitated these classes. The letters indicate which learning units can be interchanged and which ones build upon each other in a sequential way. The section entitled "Who, Me, Lead a Group?" could be regarded as a separate entity. We have placed it in the beginning of the book so that you will read it before you read the rest of the Leader Guide. It gives background information on the theory underlying the methods of facilitating learning in an adult group.

HOW TO USE THIS BOOK

Read it through to see the whole design. Collect or construct the visual materials. Gather ten to sixteen adults who are interested in building self-esteem and explore the model with them.

It has already been used with parents, teachers, adoptive parents, foster parents, grandparents, people who are not parents, social workers, and day care and health care providers. People having a wide range of educational skills have reported that by the eighth meeting they had improved their ability to nurture other people and themselves.

Remember, effective leaders don't have to be perfect. Go ahead and use the model. Don't pretend to believe something that you don't believe. If you disagree with some part of the theory, you can tell the group you disagree; do the exercises anyway, and find out what you and the group learn from the experience. Trust yourself. Celebrate the power of people to know what they need.

The plans have been refined with critical love and caring and are presented to you with the hope that they will help you in your journey.

TO THE FACILITATORS

TABLE OF CONTENTS

PREFACE   **v**

HOW TO USE THIS BOOK   **v**

WHO, ME, LEAD A GROUP?   **i**

LETTER TO MARJ 1   **29**

MEETING 1   **36**

During the first meeting the people in the group
. . . adopt *Ground Rules*
. . . examine course *Goals* and establish personal goals
. . . practice *Communication* skills
. . . learn how to help each other with problems by using a
    Suggestion Circle and a *Four Ways of Parenting* exercise
. . . compare *Beliefs* about families
. . . experience three different ways of *Inviting High Self-Esteem.*

LETTER TO MARJ 2   **55**

MEETING 2   **63**

During the second meeting the people in the group
. . . talk more about *Beliefs* about families
. . . think about what makes a person a *Good Mother* or a *Good
    Father*
. . . list *Things to Do Instead of Hitting*
. . . clarify the differences among the *Four Ways of Parenting*
. . . practice clear thinking and clear talking about who is
    Responsible for what
. . . contrast self-esteem raising messages called *Affirmations* with
    the esteem lowering messages called negations
. . . practice affirming life or *Being*
. . . examine the theory of *Recycling,* the idea that adults go
    through a constant, rhythmic pattern of growth
. . . discuss tips on *Caring for Infants*
. . . define the word *Stroke* and compare five different kinds.

LETTER TO MARJ 3   **87**

MEETING 3   **92**

During the third meeting the people in the group
. . . identify rules about giving and getting *Strokes*

. . . use jelly beans to practice giving and getting *Five Kinds of Strokes*

. . . identify *Three Parts of the Personality*

. . . share ideas about what makes a *Good Mother or a Good Father*

. . . practice *Four* different *Ways of Parenting*

. . . practice ways to encourage *Responsibility* by making clear that people, not things, are responsible for behavior

. . . practice ways to raise self-esteem at every age by *Affirming* a person's ability to develop strong internal *Structure,* morals and manners

. . . discuss ways to *Nurture Six- to Twelve-Year-Old Children.*

LETTER TO MARJ 4   113

MEETING 4   117

During the fourth meeting the people in the group

. . . practice ways to strengthen the *Problem Solving* part of the personality

. . . practice ways to invite adults to be *Responsible* for their own thoughts and feelings

. . . discuss alternative ways adults can *Respond to* angry outbursts in *Two Year Olds*

. . . compare the storage of good and bad feelings to a *Bank* balance

. . . identify ways in which people minimize or *Discount* other people or themselves

. . . examine ways that *Rules about* giving and getting *Strokes* can raise or lower self-esteem.

LETTER TO MARJ 5   137

MEETING 5   141

During the fifth meeting the people in the group

. . . review and update *Personal Goals*

. . . examine ways people can use a *Stroke Quotient* decision to lower or raise self-esteem

. . . practice *Rejecting Destructive Communications*

. . . discuss ways to foster *Spontaneity* and encourage *Socially Appropriate Behavior*

. . . consider the importance of *Separating Sex and Nurturing*

. . . practice ways to raise self-esteem by encouraging achievement, *Doing*

. . . practice ways to encourage children to be *Responsible* for their own thoughts and feelings

. . . identify ways to provide a healthy environment for *Six- to Eighteen-Month-Old Children.*

LETTER TO MARJ 6   165

MEETING 6   169

During the sixth meeting the people in the group

. . . identify *Specific Messages* that encourage or discourage high self-esteem in themselves or some person who is important to them

. . . practice *Affirmations* that encourage children to develop a strong personal identity

. . . continue to practice *Rejecting Destructive Communications*

. . . practice ways to encourage children to say no *Responsibly*

. . . discuss constructive ways of *Parenting Three- to Six-Year-Old Children.*

LETTER TO MARJ 7   187

MEETING 7   190

During the seventh meeting the people in the group

. . . review the *Three Parts of the Personality*

. . . practice *Giving and Getting Strokes* directed to each of the personality parts

. . . continue to practice indentifying and *Rejecting Communications That Are Destructive*

. . . compare the seriousness of different *Levels of Discounting*

. . . practice ways to encourage *Responsibility* by countering responses which change the meanings of communications

. . . consider ways to offer messages that *Affirm* self-esteem in teenagers as they assume new sexual roles and separate from dependence on their families

. . . discuss ways adults can help themselves and teenagers become *Separate and Independent* of each other

. . . consider becoming an *Ongoing Support Group.*

LETTER TO MARJ 8   209

MEETING 8   212

During the eighth meeting the people in the group

. . . review individual *Goals*

. . . select *Activities* from among eight options that include how to build support groups, how to strengthen a family or a group, how to assess one's current self-esteem level, and ways to extend one's support base

. . . *Celebrate* growth and create an *Affirmation* daisy for each person.

BIBLIOGRAPHY   **229**

ACKNOWLEDGMENTS   **234**

WHO, ME, LEAD A GROUP?

When people prepare to lead meetings like the ones presented in this book, they often ask questions like these:

QUESTION 1:

WHAT ARE THE QUALITIES OF AN EFFECTIVE LEADER OF ADULT LEARNING GROUPS?

QUESTION 2:

HOW DO ADULTS LEARN AND HOW CAN I FACILITATE ADULTS' LEARNING?

- What Motivates Adults to Learn?
- What Are the Steps in Adults' Learning Process?
    - Step 1   Where Adults Get Information
    - Step 2   How Adults Organize Learning Material
    - Step 3   How Adults Take in Information
    - Step 4   How Adults Start to Make Changes in Their Lives
    - Step 5   How Adults Look, Act, and Sound While They Are Learning New Skills

QUESTION 3:

HOW IS EACH MEETING DESIGNED TO HELP LEARNING HAPPEN?

QUESTION 4:

WHAT IS MY RESPONSIBILITY TO THE GROUP?

WHAT IS MY CONTRACT?

QUESTION 5:

WHAT CAN I DO TO PREPARE MYSELF?

QUESTION 6:

WHAT WILL I DO IF PROBLEMS ARISE?

QUESTION 7:

WHAT WILL I DO IF SOMEONE WANTS TO USE THE GROUP TO RESOLVE PERSONAL PROBLEMS THAT THE GROUP IS NOT EQUIPPED TO HANDLE?

QUESTION 8:

HOW DO I END THE GROUP AND HOW IMPORTANT IS CLOSURE?

QUESTION 1:

WHAT ARE THE QUALITIES OF AN EFFECTIVE LEADER OF ADULT LEARNING GROUPS?

Warmth, indirectness, cognitive organization and enthusiasm are four qualities that are found in effective leaders of adult groups.[1] Think how much of each of these qualities you already possess.

1. Warmth—Effective leaders
   - speak well of people
   - tend to like and trust rather than fear other people
   - establish warm relationships with people
2. Indirectness—Effective leaders
   - let people discover things for themselves
   - are willing to refrain from telling everything they know, even when it would be "good for people." Allan Tough found that learners preferred helpers who offered helpful resources rather than "answers."[2]
3. Cognitive Organization—Effective leaders
   - have clear behaviorial objectives in mind
   - divide learning into orderly steps
   - have knowledge well categorized so they can offer appropriate data in response to questions
   - are clear about what they know and what they don't know
   - are willing to say so and not pretend when they are in doubt
4. Enthusiasm—Effective leaders
   - feel enthusiastic about people
   - are enthusiastic about the subject matter
     Using the the scale below, rate yourself on each of these qualities. Then come back and rate yourself again after you

2

finish reading this section, "Who, Me, Lead a Group?" You may discover that you have more leadership skills than you thought you had. If you rate yourself a third time, after you lead the meetings, you may discover that you have sharpened your leadership skills considerably.

● *WARMTH*

10 9 8 7 6 5 4 3 2 1
warm, open,   cold,
friendly   closed

● *INDIRECTNESS*

10 9 8 7 6 5 4 3 2 1
helpful in allowing   eager to tell
people to discover   everything
for themselves   known

● *COGNITIVE ORGANIZATION*

10 9 8 7 6 5 4 3 2 1
clear about goals,   disorganized
well organized,   in thought
willing to   and speech
say "I don't know."

● *ENTHUSIASM*

10 9 8 7 6 5 4 3 2 1
positive about subject   flat,
matter and   passive, or
people, expressive   cynical

You may already possess an abundance of each of these qualities. You can generate your own warmth and enthusiasm. Indirectness and cognitive organization are built into the meeting plans and are explained further on pages 11-15.

QUESTION 2:

HOW DO ADULTS LEARN AND HOW CAN I FACILITATE ADULTS' LEARNING?
● WHAT MOTIVATES ADULTS TO LEARN?

Adults who want to learn are motivated in a specific or in a general way. A vague dissatisfaction and a wish to do something better are general motivations. People with general motivation say things like, "I just want to talk with other adults about what they do with a kid who has low self-esteem," or "I would like to learn to communicate better."

Specific motivations come from internal pressure generated by a specific life situation. Examples of specific motivation are: "I'm upset because my spouse and I don't agree on discipline, and I want to learn some new ways." "I don't know what to expect of a two year old, and my boy turns two next month." "I feel like hitting my child so often it scares me, and I need to learn some things to do instead." In each of these cases the learner states an internal feeling or expectation that is motivating him to learn something specific. Sometimes specific motivation to learn comes from outside the learner. The need for academic certification or pressure from a boss are examples.

People who come to meetings because they are motivated by outside pressure are often resistant learners. I do not recommend the learning meetings in this book for someone who is coming because a spouse insists, and I do not accept people in my groups whose expressed purpose in attending is to change a spouse or a coworker. This series was not designed for people to attend under duress. The meetings are invitational and rely upon self-motivation and self-evaluation. I do not expect them to be successful in institutions where attendance is mandatory or where even subtle pressure is put upon people to attend. The meetings, however, are being used in a therapeutic setting. They have become an integral part of the treatment program in the Mental Health Unit at Mercy Medical Center, Coon Rapids, Minnesota, where patients are not pressed to attend parent education class and are involved in the process of group assignments. In that setting, minister/therapist/educator Bruce Pederson successfully coleads the meetings in an ongoing cycle.

4

● WHAT ARE THE STEPS IN ADULTS' LEARNING PROCESS?

STEP 1 WHERE ADULTS GET INFORMATION

Once motivated to start toward a learning goal, adults seek help at some point. Some get information from friends or co-workers, some go to the library or find other sources of written material, some use television or other film sources, and sometimes adults attend meetings in order to learn. Adults who attend meetings often expect—

- to learn helpful concepts and skills offered by the facilitator
- to be offered visual helps such as books, charts, films
- to learn from the collective experience of the other people in the group

Since adult learners prefer to be in charge of their own learning, it is important for the facilitator —

- to present material and then leave the decision about the material and the life application up to the learners
- to be sure that the visual material is available, clear and readable
- to structure ways in which the learners can tap the resources of other people in the group

When adults attend the meetings outlined in this book, they have the help of the book *Self-Esteem: A Family Affair*, the concepts offered in the meeting plans, and the collective experience of everyone in the meetings available to them.

STEP 2 HOW ADULTS ORGANIZE LEARNING MATERIAL

Some adults organize learning material by first getting an overview of the material, a big picture, and then seeing where various parts fit in.

Some adults organize learning material in another way. They search about for bits and pieces, or even large chunks, from which they create their own view of the big picture. Other adults like both the big picture and lots of concrete pieces to fit into it.

The people who need the big picture first are often goal-oriented. They are uncomfortable being asked to do something unless there was an explanation first indicating how the activity contributes to the larger goal. They like to have the abstract theory and then the direct experience that illustrates it. They like to learn the basic principle and then how it applies. They want to hear a synopsis before they study a single scene. They are eager to get the feeling for the whole project before thay start doing the individual task. They read ahead. They feel uncomfortable when they do not know what content and methods will be included in the meetings, and they say things like:

"I really don't get it."
"I don't know what you are driving at."
"I don't understand how this fits."
"What does this have to do with me?"
"I don't see why you are going to do this."

It is as if they are not part of the learning—as if something is happening *to* them. If they don't get the structure they need to become part of the learning process, they are apt to leave.

Once they have the big picture, they join the learning process and make judgments about how individual pieces fit into the big picture. Then they say things like:

"I see how that fits."
"I think this piece makes more sense if we use it this way."
"I have an idea that relates to what we are talking about."

Now they are in charge of their learning and are helping make things happen.

People in the second group, those who like to build from small pieces, organize their learning experiences in a different way. They like to see a play without having caught the last scene on TV first; they prefer to hear a story from the beginning without being told the ending ahead of time. They are comfortable learning each step of the dance and then putting it all together. They start to assemble a toy before they read the directions. They enjoy taking a lot of direct experiences and putting them together to see if they suggest an abstract theory that will fit them all. When they aren't offered enough separate pieces or concrete experiences they say things like:

"Too much lecture."
"The explanation was too long."
"I like it better when we jump right in and do things."
"Too boring."

After they get the pieces they need, they regain their enthusiasm and make remarks such as:

"This is beginning to fit together for me."
"I like how this builds on what we did at the last meeting."
"I think I am getting the picture."
"This makes sense."
"We did something at work this week that fits in with
    something we are doing here."

Now they are in control of their learning and are contributing to the process.

Since most groups include people who want to see the big picture from the beginning, people who want to build the big picture for themselves, and people who want some of both, be sure to—

- state the goals for each meeting clearly and post or hand out a printed sheet
- present separate pieces of information clearly

Besides the fact that some people prefer to start learning experiences with abstract theories or big pictures and other people prefer to start learning with smaller pieces, there is another reason for the facilitator to take care to include both theory and experience for each learning objective: People do not use abstract theory to change behavior until they translate the theories into concrete experiences. Conversely, learning from one concrete experience is not transferred to another experience until the learning has been related to some abstract theory or made symbolic. The words "love for all humankind" are symbols. They represent an abstract theory. They are, in fact, carbon on cellulose. The person who writes about the importance of love for all humankind and beats the four year old who interrupts the writing hasn't connected the symbols with the experience. Not until the person has connected those symbols with some concrete love experiences such as willingly caring for a child, or experiencing unexpected help from a stranger, can the person start to behave in ways that express love for all humankind. On the other hand, the adult who devotes time and energy to providing tender, loving nurturing for one child and sees no need to spend tax dollars installing a traffic light at a hazardous school crossing hasn't connected the isolated concrete experience of expressing love to a child with the theory of love of children.

Each of these eight meeting plans relates new theory to the overall goals. Theories are presented briefly and are followed by specific activities that illustrate concrete ways in which the theory can be experienced in daily behavior. For example, in Meeting 3, the leader explains one part of the theory that words can encourage or discourage responsible behavior. The leader says "One way to encourage responsibility in children and in ourselves is to remember that things and situations are not responsible for behavior; people are responsible for behavior." That is followed by the Things are Falling into Place exercise, which gives people a chance to examine and rewrite common communications. Then people are asked to notice whether they use words at home that invite irresponsibility, and if so, to consider substituting other words.

Therefore, in order to honor the various ways in which adults organize learning materials, it is important at every meeting for the facilitator to—

- present the theory clearly
- point out how the new theory relates to the overall goals
- include the specific activities that illustrate concrete ways in which the theories can be experienced and evaluated in daily behavior

STEP 3 HOW ADULTS TAKE IN INFORMATION

You are ready to present abstract theories and concrete experience. How will you do that?

Adults seem to get most of their information in four ways: through their eyes, their ears, their bodies, and their intuition. Some adults use all four.

Some people have a strong preference for taking information through their eyes, or visually. They like to read, to look at people when they talk, to see pictures, diagrams and charts, to watch films. They turn on the light before they answer the phone. They say things like:

"I'll look into it."

"I'll see what I can do."

"Look sharp."

"Are you beginning to see the light?"

Some people prefer to collect information through their ears, or audibly. They would rather listen to the news on the radio than look at the newspaper. They are uncomfortable when background noise is so high it interferes with the auditory cues they are accustomed to depending on. They would rather listen to a story than read it. They use tape cassettes or CB radios to collect information while they are driving. They would rather have verbal directions to a friend's house than use a map or follow the road signs. They say things like:

"Tell you what I'll do."

"Lend me your ear."

"Now listen, here is the word!"

Other adults learn best with their bodies, or kinesthetically. They like to "walk through things." They are impatient with lectures and they move their toes and their fingers while they think. They like to go for long walks to think things over, or they make decisions while they are jogging. While they think, they may "walk purposefully" around a room in a way that is different from "anxiously pacing." They say things like:

"I'll run through some possible solutions in my mind."

"Let's find out if anyone came up with a new idea."

"I think I have a handle on it now."

Taste and smell are important ways in which people can collect information, but these ways are often discounted or ignored when planning group learning experiences, except in food and beverage preparation classes. How much do you think the learning in a group is affected if the room smells fresh or musty, or has the lingering odor of lilacs or of over-used kitty litter?

Many learners do not depend on one sense but like to use all of their senses to collect information. Maybe these are the people who are most intuitive.

So what is the leader's responsibility to provide for the different ways adults take in information? Leaders should remember that no matter what their personal learning style preferences are, the following elements are important:

- attractive, readable visuals
- clear spoken messages
- learning exercises that involve moving the body
- adequate ventilation

These are all significant ways to facilitate the learning experiences in groups.

One way to be sure that a variety of senses is stimulated is to identify the body involvement in each separate learning experience. I identify learning units on a check sheet to be sure that I am not appealing too greatly to any one sense. Repeatedly I notice that the learning units that get the best responses in the group are the ones that show marks all across the page. The sample on page 25 shows a listing for Meeting 3.

STEP 4 HOW ADULTS START TO MAKE CHANGES IN THEIR LIVES

When people make changes in their lives in a certain area, they may start by changing the way they talk about that subject, how they act about it, their attitude toward it, or an underlying decision concerning it.

Let us say that you are facilitating a group in which Julia has announced that she is going to stop spanking as a method of discipline. Julia can start to make this change in her life by first changing her words, her attitudes, her behavior, or her basic decision.

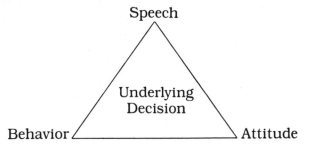

Julia may take the first step by changing the way she speaks about her child. She will say, "Logan needs discipline," instead of "Logan needs a spanking." Or Julia could take the first step by changing her behavior. When she feels like spanking Logan she will move him off to sit in the corner instead.

She could examine her ideas of discipline and change her attitude from a flippant "Spare the rod and spoil the child," to a thoughtful "It is my responsibility to socialize my child without using violence."

Julia may even change an underlying decision. Suppose, for example, she had accepted the idea that women are powerless. She, therefore, did not expect and demand certain behaviors from Logan but let him do whatever he wanted. When his behavior became intolerable to her, she hit him. After Julia changes her belief about herself as a woman, claims her power and her ability to model, she expects and demands appropriate social behavior. Logan's behavior improves so that she no longer finds it intolerable, and therefore she doesn't spank.

If any one of these four changes (speech, action, attitude, or underlying decision) is made deliberately and conscientiously and consistently, in time, the others will usually follow.

STEP 5 HOW ADULTS LOOK, ACT, AND SOUND WHILE THEY ARE LEARNING NEW SKILLS

While they are making changes and practicing new skills, many adults look and feel awkward. As they practice and refine the new skill, they become graceful. Other adults seem to burst forth with new behavior as suddenly as if they had put on a new hat and the hat had changed the way they walked. Often those people are not exhibiting behavior that they decided to change only a minute ago, but are showing the results of a period of thought, decision, or practice in fantasy. It is as if they had gone through the awkward period internally or in private. It is probable that all adults experience some awkwardness while learning a new skill, just as children do. Some adults find learning new skills exciting and don't mind the clumsiness; others confuse awkwardness with insincerity and feel tempted to stop practicing the new behavior. They may say something like, "I want to give more compliments, but I just didn't sound sincere; so I stopped doing it. I'm afraid my voice sounds phony."

Therefore, it is important to create a climate in the meetings where—
- people get support for achievement
- it is safe for people to practice
- it is safe for people to be awkward

• it is safe for people to try out a new behavior before they choose to keep or to discard it

QUESTION 3:

HOW IS EACH MEETING DESIGNED TO HELP LEARNING HAPPEN?

Warmth, enthusiasm, indirectness and cognitive organization are the four qualities of an effective teacher of adults. You may say, "I'll bring the warmth and enthusiasm, but what about indirectness and cognitive organization?" Indirectness and cognitive organization are built into the learning activities in the meeting plans of this manual.

INDIRECTNESS

Indirectness is allowing people to discover for themselves what they need, rather than insisting that they learn what you think is good for them.

There is an old adage about teaching that says, "First you tell them what you are going to teach them, then you teach them, then you tell them what you taught them." Right? No, not if you are teaching adults! That direct teaching is called *pedagogy.* It is the way most children are taught.

Adults prefer to learn indirectly, to have an active part in the goal setting and in the process of the learning situation, and to reach their own conclusions. The new adage is—
• first you and they set the goals
• then you tell them briefly what you have to offer and how it relates to the goals
• then you provide the opportunity for them to experience and share
• then you ask them what they learned

You are responsible for the teaching and the structure, but you cannot control what people learn, what insights they glean. For you to set learning goals for people discounts their ability to learn what they need to learn for themselves. It is patronizing or "one-up" teaching. If you insist upon trying to control the learning, you teach that people must give the response you want or suffer negative consequences. When that happens, people are displaying compliant behavior, and you do not know what personal learnings or insights they have gained. Their learnings may have been the opposite of your teaching goals.

If I insist that Fred solve a discipline problem in the way that I am convinced is best, what Fred may learn is that my way is confusing to him, that he doesn't know how he will manage the discipline, but that he surely will do it differently from the way that I dictated. When you remember that people will discover what is useful for them at the given moment, not necessarily what you want them to discover, you will be on the road to indirectness.

Read through each meeting carefully and mark the places where people are encouraged to discover for themselves. If you want to do additional reading about indirect teaching you can read *The Modern Practice of Adult Education: Andragogy Versus Pedagogy* by Malcolm Knowles.[3] In it he describes *andragogy*, the act and science of facilitating adult learning. It differs from pedagogy, which is the teacher-directed learning that many of us experienced in our own school years. For those of us who have a tendency to fall back into pedagogy, thoughtful consideration and practice of the various elements of andragogy can dramatically improve our ability to teach adults. Knowles suggests, among other things, that facilitators of adult learning provide indirectness by—

- mutually negotiating objectives
- giving adults chances to learn from each other
- using experiential (doing) techniques as well as transmitting (telling) techniques
- providing an informal, respectful, collaborative climate

In this manual, *mutual negotiation of objectives* for the set of meetings is structured into the first meeting, and participants are invited to add goals at the beginning of each meeting. They are also asked to rethink their goals for the course in the fifth meeting. In the meeting plans, the regular use of such exercises as the Suggestion Circle and the Four Ways of Parenting insure that people have a *chance to learn from each other* in response to needs expressed by participants and the leader. A variety of *experiential techniques* are offered for each meeting. The five ground rules built into the meeting plans in this book assure a climate that is *informal, respectful, and collaborative.*

GROUND RULES FOR PROTECTION AND PERMISSION

The ground rules are basic to the success of the meetings. Consistently used, these rules provide protection and permission for people to make their own decisions to grow. They assure a safe place for people to try new behaviors, to change their words, to consider their attitudes, and to think about their underlying beliefs. They provide a framework for indirectness. They define people as having worth and protect them from embarrassment if they make mistakes. These are important conditions for people who want to improve self-esteem. The ground rules are—

1. everyone participates
2. everyone has the right to pass
3. all opinions are honored
4. confidentiality is maintained
5. leader stays in a position of respect for self and others

The facilitator thinks about these ground rules and how he could use them to provide protection for people to grow.

1. The *Full Participation* ground rule, the assumption that everyone including the leader will mentally participate in each activity, protects the participants from being asked to do something that the leader is not willing to do.

2. The *Right to Pass* protects each individual, including the leader, from having to speak out, from revealing himself when he isn't willing to do so.

3. *Honoring* each person's attitudes, opinions, and beliefs emphasizes that they have helped him make sense out of life and therefore they have personal validity. It also affirms adults' ability to think and to decide for themselves. In addition, it protects the group from the competitiveness of having to decide who is right or wrong when people disagree.

4. The fourth ground rule of *Confidentiality*, or no gossip, provides protection for people to role play new behavior and then to decide if they want to keep or to discard it. It also encourages people to solve problems they may have with the group within the group.

5. The fifth ground rule, that the leader is expected to stay in a position of *Respect* for self and others during the meetings, protects the participants from criticism and protects the integrity of the leader. The leader is free to express her own belief position but is not to push it on other people or to apologize for it in order to please the group. This ground rule is also important because it demands that the leader model respectful, accepting behavior for the group.

It does not assume that every behavior is all right but rather that the *needs* of each person are important. For example, the leader will not allow anyone to hurt someone else but will respect that person's need for attention. And she can offer him the option of doing a Four Ways of Parenting exercise or a Suggestion Circle on his problems at each meeting.

Three of these ground rules, Full Participation, Right to Pass, and the Honoring of Everyone's Opinions and Beliefs are borrowed from the methods used in Values Clarification. If you have not been exposed to this large collection of activities designed to encourage people to clarify their own values for themselves, Kirschenbaum's and Simon's book *Readings in Values Clarification* is a helpful introduction.[4] Many of the activities in the meeting plans are Values Clarification exercises. They create time and space for people to identify and consider their own values and beliefs in a protected environment.

COGNITIVE ORGANIZATION

All right, you say, I have warmth and enthusiasm. I will use the ground rules and other indirect learning techniques that are built into the meetings. But how will I know that I have cognitive organization? There are three essential tasks in cognitive organization:

- to set clear, behavioral objectives
- to divide the learning experiences into manageable steps
- to arrange the steps to build upon each other in an orderly way

The first task of cognitive organization is to set clear behavioral objectives. The objectives for this series of meetings are stated for the whole course and for each meeting. The overall objective of these meetings is to present ideas and tools that people can consider, try out, and evaluate for improving self-esteem in their own families.

The leader's objectives are stated briefly at the start of each meeting for the people who like to see the day's activities in terms of the big picture. Example: "We will identify three ways of inviting high self-esteem." At the beginning of individual exercises, specific goals are expanded. Example: "We offer our children high self-esteem when we give them positive messages about what they do and who they are. In this exercise we will practice three ways to do that."

At the first meeting people are asked to state their own objectives for the course. Some adults are clear and specific about what they want. "I want to learn how to set limits about bedtime and succeed in setting them." Others are vague at the beginning of the meetings. "I think I'm a soft touch." Leaders can encourage people to clarify their goals as the course progresses. By the last meeting adults can articulate clearly what they have learned. For example, a parent may say, "Learning the difference between Nurturing and Structuring has been the most helpful part of these meetings for me. I wasn't sure that I had authority as a parent. Now I am setting limits for my children without criticizing or being vindictive." At each meeting participants are invited to add personally important objectives such as celebrations or problems. The leader can help them set clear goals.

14

Let us say that Bob has asked for some help. He is worried because his ten-year-old daughter is irresponsible. Since that is a vague request, the leader will help Bob clarify what he wants. "Bob, do you want help with your worrying or with ways to encourage responsible behavior?" "I want her to be responsible and I would like some ideas about how to get her to make her bed." A behavioral objective is: "Make a list of things Bob can do to encourage his ten-year-old daughter to make her bed."

Following is a list of direct, measurable action words that are helpful in writing clear, behavioral objectives. Robert Mager's small book *Goal Analysis*[5] offers further help in writing clear objectives.

Direct Measurable Action Words

draw	fill out	illustrate	isolate
collect	select	examine	design
change	find	compile	evaluate
change from/to	acquire	select	relate
tell	obtain	categorize	investigate
share	memorize	rank order	analyze
interview	present	conduct	compare
read	prepare	organize	contrast
discuss	define	develop	edit
write	describe	explain	invent
list	identify		

The second task of cognitive organization is to divide learning experiences into manageable steps. This implies the development and use of a firm theory foundation and the division of learning tasks so they make sense to the learner.

The theoretical foundation for these meeting plans is Transactional Analysis, a psychological and group process system devised by Eric Berne,[6] that explains attitudes and behavior in familiar terms. People who know a great deal about Transactional Analysis often enjoy the chance to rethink and to practice the theories in this setting.

People who have not been exposed to Transactional Analysis do not have difficulty following the material presented in these meetings. The theories are presented indirectly, through exercises, to be discovered and tested by the learners.

The learning experiences have been divided into manageable steps. For example, the first time the Four Ways of Parenting exercise is presented, people are invited to read role examples from the book. At the second meeting, people practice identifying the qualities of each role. In later meetings, after people are familiar with the four roles, they make up their own responses to problems.

The third task of cognitive organization is to arrange the steps to build upon each other in an orderly way. The steps in this model are arranged in a way that is designed to be non-threatening and to invite people to build upon their strengths.

A detailed description of the theoretical base used in the sequencing is described in the chapter on self-esteem in *Family Strengths: Positive Models for Family Life.*[7]

QUESTION 4:

WHAT IS MY RESPONSIBILITY TO THE GROUP? WHAT IS MY CONTRACT?

Leaders of groups are generally familiar with the contracts they need with employers or sponsoring institutions. What exchange of money is involved? How is the class advertised? Who opens the room? Do I turn off the lights and lock up? Do we serve coffee? Who makes it? Who pays for it? Who cleans up? Who evaluates my work? How?

Leaders also make contracts, explicit or implicit, with their groups. I have attended groups where the only contract that is discussed between a leader and the group members is the exchange of money. "How much and when do I pay? Or get paid?" I believe that there are many more elements in the contract a leader has with a group. The following contract items are implicit in these meetings plans, and the success of the groups will be affected by how carefully the leader observes these contracts.

Item 1. The leader *provides structure* —

a. by doing his homework—by being thoroughly acquainted with the meeting plans, both the cognitive and the experiential part of the design

b. by taking charge of the setting—by attending to temperature and fresh air, by insisting that outside distractions not interfere with the flow of the meetings, by arranging furniture so that people are sitting comfortably, close to each other with no one outside the circle, and with no tables in front of people

c. by managing the mechanics in a way that shows respect for learners, by attending to the visual learners with posters large enough for everyone to read, to the auditory learners by making sure the acoustics are suitable, to the kinesthetic learners by attending to the movement part of the activities and by providing any props needed to assist that learning process

d. by starting and ending on time.

Item 2. The leader contracts to *trust adults to make their own decisions* and to refrain from telling people what to decide or from thinking she has to know all the answers. She expects to learn from and with the group.

Item 3. The leader contracts to *offer tools*, not to solve people's problems *for* them. Sometimes it is difficult to know whether we are helping people solve their own problems and become more self-sufficient or are taking care of people in a way that undercuts their competence and encourages them to be dependent. If a leader has a question about whether she is helping or inviting dependence about a particular problem, she can ask the following questions:
a. did the person ask me for help?
b. did the person work at least as hard at finding a solution as I did?
c. did the person say "Thank you?"
d. did I feel comfortable (not resentful) about giving help?
e. was there a cut-off date on the aid—a time when the person would assume full responsibility for this problem?
If the answer to two or more of the questions is "no," it is time for the facilitator to refocus on creating a situation where people can solve their own problems.[8]

Item 4. The leader *provides protection for group members* by scrupulously observing the ground rules. The leader *protects herself* by setting the rules that she needs for her to function well. For example, she can refuse to admit new members after the second meeting. She may choose not to lead a group with fewer than ten members because the group interaction is not sufficiently diverse. She may set her top enrollment at sixteen, or whatever number she handles well. If she judges a group to be a closed system, people who know each other very well and already have functioning group norms that would make it difficult to follow the ground rules, she may agree to work with that group only if they add an equal number of strangers. If she works more comfortably with people outside their family system, she may request spouses to work in different groups. (Often, when a husband and wife are in the same group, one of them will take care of the other by being quiet or one will protect him- or herself by not participating.) If the facilitator likes working directly with the family system, she will request the couple to take the class together. She may protect herself from inviting dependency and from the demands of scheduling by working with a team teacher so she can have less work and more fun and sometimes miss a meeting.

Item 5. The leader contracts to run a growth group, not a

therapy group. See Question 7, "What will I do if someone wants to use the group to resolve personal problems?"

Item 6. If some of the people in the group have "special contracts," the leader will make clear commitments about those at the first meeting. Perhaps someone wants to take the class for special credit. She says, "You want to use this class for special credit? Here is what I expect you to do. . . Here is what I am willing to do. . . ."

QUESTION 5:

WHAT CAN I DO TO PREPARE MYSELF?

Who takes care of the leader? The leader does, that's who, and you can take care of yourself in the following ways:
- Prepare, become thoroughly familiar with your plans. Practice parts or all of them aloud, or with a co-leader. Have an internal conversation with the Letters to Marj.
- Take time for yourself. Schedule adequate time for rest, food, and contemplation before the meetings. Poor grooming discounts you as well as the people you work with, so spend some time on yourself. You deserve it!
- Practice what you promote. Visualize yourself as the warm, enthusiastic, competent, dynamic leader you are becoming. Get affirmations before the class. If it isn't possible to get them from other people, make a tape of the messages you need to hear and listen to it before each meeting. Affirm yourself. Write out the Affirmations that will help you lead and say them to yourself five times on the way to the meeting. For example:
    "I am a competent, warm, caring, intuitive leader."
    "I think well on my feet."
    "I listen to what people want and need."
    "I provide firm but flexible structure."
    "I am lucky to have this opportunity, and these people are lucky to work with me."
    "I enjoy leading this group."
- Separate your own feelings, thinking, and beliefs. Claim your beliefs; affirm your ability to think and take care of your feelings. If you feel hurt by criticism from group members, learn to hear the kernel of truth that is in the criticism and use it to improve your facilitating ability. Let the bad feelings go.
    If you are comfortable only with "either-or" answers,

practice looking for five possibilities rather than settling for "either-or" solutions. If you want a gold star for leading a group where everyone agrees, get help! Get a box of gold stars and give them to yourself free. You don't have to earn them by having people agree with you—you have already earned them by being willing to lead indirectly and to encourage people to come to their own conclusions.

- Be aware that you set the tone for the meeting during the first three minutes. Before you enter the meeting, get in touch with your own warmth and enthusiasm and remember that the class is lucky to have a caring leader like you. You start the meeting from the moment you see the first person. Forget to say negatives like, "I don't know if I can do this," and do say positives like, "I'm glad to be here. This will be an interesting session."
- Remember, it is OK to have fun while you facilitate.

QUESTION 6:

WHAT WILL I DO IF PROBLEMS ARISE?

If a problem arises, identify it, think and feel what you need to do to resolve it.

Whose problem is it? If it is yours, you can fix that. If it is the group's, go back and renegotiate the contract—you are there to offer tools; it is up to them to accept or reject.

PROBLEM: GROUP DYNAMICS

Is the meeting dragging? Speed it up—you are responsible for pace. Is the energy low? Keep the meeting moving. Check the temperature and ventilation; the room may be hot and stuffy. Are the chairs comfortable? Does the setting encourage alertness? Small chairs or bean bag chairs encourage bodies to double over and energy to lower.

Are you working too hard? A leader who tries hard to answer every question discourages other people from thinking. Are you working with too small a group? You may need more people for greater interaction. Or are there too many people? See if you can split the group or divide it for some tasks.

Are people not talking? Check yourself to be sure that when you ask a question you make eye contact with several people and wait for an answer. Follow the ground rules. Insist that each answer be treated with respect. Honor "passing," and use it yourself sometimes.

Do one or two people talk all the time, dominate the group with laughter or sarcasm, or use group time to try to fix other people's problems? Insist on the use of the ground rules and on staying with the tasks at hand. Use the Suggestion Circle or the Four Ways of Parenting, and move along! Are husband and wife using the meetings to try to change each other? Remind them that these tools are designed to help them impact their family's self-esteem by changing themselves.

PROBLEM: TIME

Is the group not covering the meeting plans in the time alloted? Do what works. If the group finishes early, OK, but don't run overtime. Either speed up or ask the group to extend the meeting times. Some groups like to spend two hours on these meetings; others prefer two and one-half or three. The time depends on you and the pace of the group. *Do not bunch the meetings into a weekend.* Most of the learning takes place between meetings. These were designed with between-meeting assignments to do, practice, and contemplate. If you cram them into a weekend, that built-in learning experience will be lost.

PROBLEM: INDIVIDUALS

Someone complains that a learning experience is phony, insincere. Remind her of the right to pass. Remind her to separate awkwardness and insincerity. Someone says "Why all the exercises? I'm not learning anything. Where is the meat in the course?" Remind her of the right to pass. Remind her that some people learn faster by doing than from lecture. Invite her to read the books listed in the bibliography.

If someone says, "Too much theory—I like it when we do things," remind him of the right to pass. Remind him that people's learning styles differ, and some people learn more quickly if they grasp theory first. Check yourself to see if you are thinking for people—spoon-feeding. Listen for kernels of truth, but make your own judgments.

Is someone continually saying "Yes, but . . ." or "But don't you think that. . . ." and pulling the group off on a tangent? Don't answer "Yes, but. . . ." Get one round of suggestions from the group and then move on. Invite the "Don't you think" person to say what he thinks, honor it, and then go on with the meeting.

If someone criticizes you severely, do not respond. Saying "I resent your saying that" invites her to fight. Explaining or defending puts you on the defensive. You are not obliged to make any immediate response to resentments except to listen and to think. Look for the kernel of truth and change your behavior if

20

that is appropriate. Ask for Resentments and Appreciations at the end of every meeting.

Does someone stay after the meeting to criticize what you did during the meeting? "You were awful at first, but I'm glad I gave you another chance. You turned out not to be as bad as I thought. Let me tell you how you can improve." Leave. Do not listen, This is crooked criticizing. The place for resentments is during Resentments and Appreciations.

Does someone push you during every meeting? When you fix one thing, does he push on something else? Some people push. If you fix the whole world, they will still push you for not having fixed the moon and the stars. You choose which pushes to respond to and how much.

PROBLEM: YOU

Do you have difficulty accepting personal challenges? Practice alternatives at home and use a response at the meetings that respects both the other person and yourself. Be sincere. Someone says, "I think you are phony when you say you are glad I am here. Last meeting I didn't think you acted glad."

Do not take responsibility for the other person's discomfort and offer to change yourself to please her. Do not say, "I'm sorry you feel that way, and I want you to believe that I am really glad to see you, and I wouldn't say that if I weren't, and if it bothers you that I said that, I will not say anything like that again, and you be sure to tell me if you are uncomfortable with my words and I will change them."

Do not be defensive. Avoid "I'm really upset that you feel that way and what can I do to prove to you that I am sincere, because I really am sincere!"

Do not attack. Avoid "Well, I'm trying to stay glad that you are here, but it's hard.'"

Do not be vindictive. Avoid "Look, it really doesn't make any difference to me whether you think I am sincere or not!"

Do not placate. Avoid "I can see why you would feel that way and I'm glad you told me. Just stick around and I will try to prove to you that I am glad."

Do stay respectful of self and others. Say, "I accept that you think I am not sincere. In fact, I have looked forward to working with this group for a long time and I feel glad that you are here, but it is OK with me if you don't believe that." And go on with the meeting.

PROBLEM: YOUR LEADERSHIP SKILLS

Do you have difficulty getting people to think for themselves? Listen to the words you use when you invite people to think.

Do not say "Would you . . .?" That is an invitation for the learner to please you instead of thinking for himself.

Do not say "What I want you to do is . . . ." That is a worse statement than "Would you . . .?"

Do not say "Could you . . .?" This implies that the leader doesn't have power.

Do not say "I was just going to say, could you . . .?" This is even more powerless.

Do not say "Why don't you . . .?" This is a secret message that they certainly ought to.

Do not say "Now you will . . . ." This is an invitation to rebellion.

Say "Will you . . .?" This leaves them free to say yes or no or to pass.

PROBLEM: NOT ENOUGH JOY

If you are not having as much fun leading as you want—

- Ask for extra appreciations at the beginning and at the end.
- Get a team leader, nurture each other, problem solve together, have fun together. While you are leading, ask each other for help, respect each other's opinions and skills, and interrupt each other with ideas and facts, but do not interrupt in a way that distracts the other person's thinking.
- Remember, it is OK to enjoy the group. Honor their knowledge, share yours, learn from them and laugh with them.

QUESTION 7:

WHAT WILL I DO IF SOMEONE WANTS TO USE THE GROUP TO RESOLVE PERSONAL PROBLEMS IN A WAY THAT THE GROUP IS NOT EQUIPPED TO HANDLE?

Is there someone in the group who wants to do therapy? If that someone is you and you are a therapist, stop leading this learning group and lead a therapy group. Otherwise, you can refer that person for counseling or therapy. When do you refer someone for therapy? I don't know when *you* should, but I can tell you when *I* do. When I observe a person who is exhibiting emotions that seem to be grossly out of proportion to the situation, I tell the person my observations and ask if he or she is interested in getting some help. If the person says yes, I suggest places to go for help. I refer only people who want to change, since therapy doesn't do anything *to* people, it only gives them new tools to do something *for themselves.* I find no point in referring people who want to stay where they are.

If you want to lead a learning or growth group, how can you keep from wandering over into therapy? Since there is some learning in therapy and some therapy in learning, there's not a clear-cut line between them. I use the following five questions to help me differentiate:

1. How are the individual's problems or disruptive behavior approached? The learning group addresses a problem in a way that furthers the learning goals of the whole group. Example: "Would you like us to practice Four Ways of Parenting for that problem?" The therapy group looks for the roots of the problem and how it can be resolved at that level. Example: "When was the first time you had that problem?"

2. What is the focus of the group activity? The focus in a learning group is on skills the whole group can use. Example: "If you are willing, we can use the criticism you describe as an example when we practice Rejecting Toxic Strokes later in this meeting." The focus in a therapy group is on how the individual functions. Example: "What benefit do you get out of accepting a criticism like that?"

3. When is feedback given? In a learning group, feedback is given when asked for. Example: "Did I do that correctly?" "Not quite. Try it again and this time . . . ." In therapy, feedback is given routinely. Example: "What is going on with your feet? You have been moving them all the time you were talking."

4. What are the primary objectives of the group? The objectives of a learning group are to acquire new understandings, skills, and behaviors. Example: "You seem to be especially interested in this topic. Do you want us to run through it again with a different example?" The goal of a therapy group is to resolve the individual's personal problems by resolving the hidden motivations. Example: "When we talk about feelings you start a conversation about something else. What's going on with you?" Personal behavior change comes from both groups.

5. How does the role of the leader differ in the two groups? The leader of a learning group looks for positives to build on, functions as a facilitator, focuses on group process and tasks, directs and coordinates activities, intervenes when behavior interferes with the group tasks, and deals with the here and now. The therapist looks for positives to build on, confronts negatives, focuses on individual needs, interprets interactions and motivations, intervenes to interpret the meaning of behavior, and deals with the present and the past.

Some people feel a warning, a body tightening, when a learning group is getting into personal therapy issues. I believe that when the leader is certain about the purpose of a learning group, the therapy issue is less apt to arise.

QUESTION 8:

HOW DO I END THE GROUP AND HOW IMPORTANT IS CLOSURE?

"All's well that ends well" may not always be true, but nothing good can be said for sloppy endings. End each meeting on time; end each meeting on a positive note. Do an affirming closing experience at each meeting. If you run short of time and have to skip or postpone something, do not let it be the Affirmations. They are the positives, the messages that encourage people to grow, to be, to do.

If, after the last of a series of meetings, the group will meet again in some other way, get careful closure on this series anyway. A feeling that loose ends have not been attended to can invite people to discount positive gains they have made. Encourage people to count their wins at the final meeting. You count your successes. Claim the personal growth you made as you moved with this group through these meetings. Count the skills you have achieved as a competent, effective facilitator of adult learning. Claim your warmth, your enthusiasm, your ability to lead indirectly and your skill at cognitive organization. Celebrate your wins!

	Listening	Seeing	Talking	Writing or holding an object	Moving	Moving into a group
1. Name Tag	●	●	●	●		
2. Ground Rules	●	●			●	
3. Goals	●	●	●			
4. Stroke Rules	●		●	●		
5. Jelly Bean	●	●	●			●
6. Three Personality Parts	●	●	●		●	
7. Nurturing & Structuring	●	●	●	●		●
8. Four Ways of Parenting	●	●	●		●	
9. Responsibility	●	●	●	●		●
10. Affirmations	●	●		●		●
11. Parenting Tips	●	●	●			
12. Closing	●	●	●		●	

25

INFORMATION GRID Content for each meeting is listed horizontally.

MEETING	FOUR WAYS OF PARENTING	RESPONSIBILITY AND COMMUNICATIONS	PARENTING TIPS
1	Introduction and practice	Back-to-back eye level	
2	Card review and practice	Who is responsible for what "Eggs"	0 to 6 months
3	Description and practice	People, not things, are responsible "Things are falling into place"	6 years to 12 years
4	Practice	Be responsible for self "Eat your beans for Mommy"	18 months to 3 years
5	Practice	Don't think & feel for others "You are going to love this"	6 months to 18 months
6	Practice	Say no straight "I'll do it later"	3 years to 6 years
7	Practice	Don't switch the meaning "Where are your boots?	13 years to 19 years
8	Practice		

Content areas that are developed from meeting to meeting are listed vertically.

AFFIRMATIONS	PERSONALITY PARTS	STROKES	DISCOUNT
		Three that raise self-esteem	
Being		Definition Five kinds	
Structure	Nurturing & Structuring	Practice giving & receiving or rejecting five kinds	
Thinking	Problem Solving	Bank Rules	Definition Three things discounted
Doing	Spontaneous & Adaptive	Quotient Center to reject toxics	Review
Identity & Power	Review	Buffet Reject toxics three ways	
Separation & Sexuality	Identify own today	Fair Practice rejecting toxics	Four modes or levels
Daisy Celebration	Five Dot exercise	Self-esteem today (review rules) Extend stroke base	

Notes

1. Nathaniel Lee Gage, *Teacher Effectiveness and Teacher Training: The Search for a Scientific Basis* (Palo Alto, Calif.: Pacific Books, 1972).
2. Allan Tough, *The Adult's Learning Projects* (Toronto: Ontario Institute for Studies in Education, 1975).
3. Malcolm Knowles, *The Modern Practice of Adult Education* (New York: Association Press, 1970).
4. Sidney B. Simon and Howard Kirschenbaum, *Readings in Values Clarification* (Minneapolis: Winston Press, 1973).
5. Robert F. Mager, *Goal Analysis* (Belmont, Calif.: Fearson Publishers, 1972).
6. Eric Berne, M.D., *The Structure and Dynamics of Organizations and Groups* (New York: Grove Press, 1963).
7. Dr. Nick Stinnett et al, *Family Strengths* (Lincoln, Nebraska: University of Nebraska Press, 1980).

LETTER TO MARJ 1

Dear Marj,

About the first meeting—I hope that you will enjoy it. Usually people get actively involved in the back-to-back interview, and sometimes people report that they made a new friend during the experience. This exercise is the heart of the first meeting—it lets everyone participate very early in the class. When people move and interact with a person they choose, the energy and excitement in the room are higher than if people sit still.

Let me walk through the first meeting with you. Winston Press and I agreed to avoid his/her pronoun designations, so I will alternate he and she by meetings in my writing—you may have all men, all women, or both in your meetings.

Start on time, even if everyone is not there. The **bookkeeping** involves routine business for the start of a class, but the way in which you do it sets the tone for the workshop, so be fully there— talk with people, let them know you. Many people make lasting judgments about a class or workshop based on the way the leader presents herself during the first three minutes, and your first three minutes start when people walk through the door. Have the chairs arranged in a circle to signal that people will talk with each other during these meetings. **Names.** Be sure to wear a name tag yourself. Your name is important. **Goals.** Check your posters from across the room to be sure that all words are readable. I recommend clear letters and lots of color. Posting the goals offers structure for people who like to know what is going on. It also offers visual stimulation for people who learn more easily by reading than by listening. If someone has an urgent problem, I change the order and do the **Four Ways of Parenting** or **Suggestion Circle** first.

1. This is the meeting at which you establish the **Ground Rules** and atmosphere. The ground rules are designed to set an open, protected atmosphere, and it is important that they be followed carefully by the facilitators. It is not unusual for people to wait three or four meetings before believing the ground rules; so feel free to take the right to pass yourself when you want. Do intervene if someone is making a judgment about someone else's opinion. Remind people that the ground rules give everyone the right to state an opinion or belief and have it respected as valid for that person today. The ground rules also protect *you* and set the stage for you to participate and grow with the class. They invite each person to be responsible for her own opinions and actions.

About staying in the position of Respect for Self and Others: Recently I slipped and said something to a man that was a put-down. I didn't catch myself at the time. Three meetings later he told me about it. That gave me the chance to apologize to him and to the class. Now I affirm myself before the class and that helps me maintain a position of mutual respect. I'll include some affirmations as a postscript to this letter, and you are welcome to use or to adapt them.

Generally people like the Confidentiality rule. It means "No Gossip." It is good for me because sometimes I would like to babble about what went on in class. Ask for agreement on this ground rule; it is the only one that extends outside of class. There is more about ground rules in "Who, Me, Lead a Group?" pages 12, 13, and 14.

2. Get to know members' **names** and **goals.** Do share your personal goals or wants! For example, a goal such as "To get to know some new people, to have fun, to improve my own skills in working with groups" helps people see you as a real person. A goal like "To impress my boss with my group work skills" allows people to see you as a person who has figured out a way to get her needs met. Often a group will be very supportive of a goal like this and will give suggestions for making the course better.

Goal sharing is a good time to emphasize the importance of people using this class to look at themselves. Any idea or concept can be misused, and it would be unfortunate if anyone took home the ideas taught in this course and used them as clubs over other people. We should all avoid saying "I learned in class today that everyone needs blah, blah, blah, and you never blah, blah, blah, and furthermore the last time you blah, blah, blah." I tell people that if they are going to make someone else take the course by going home and telling them what to do, they must pay tuition for that person.

Sometimes people are reluctant to state their own goals or wishes. They may not know exactly what these are, or they may have experienced being asked for their goals and then having them ignored. This is one reason why it is important to record goals and wishes. It will be easier to refer back to them during Meetings 5 and 8 and to be honest about the ones that will not be met in class.

As I listen to people's goals and wishes, I find it important for me to remember that I am not there to "fix" people but to create time and space and opportunities for them to think about what they want to do for themselves.

Sometimes during the introductions someone will make a strong plea for the whole group to focus on her problem immediately and to spend lots of time on her. There may be situations where this is appropriate, but I have not found one. If the problem is a severe personal one, a counseling or therapy referral is in order. Otherwise you can use the **Suggestion Circle** or the **Four Ways of Parenting** exercise. That will offer the group ways to express care, respond to a personal problem, and still get on with the class.

The differences between growth groups and therapy groups are discussed in "Who, Me, Lead a Group?" Allowing the group to slide into addressing archaic issues, such as "Jane, were you afraid of anger when you were little?" or giving unsolicited feedback, like "John, your neck got red when you talked about your son," breaks the contract for the class and the trust. The ground rules are designed to give people protection in a growth setting.

3. I hope you participate in the back-to-back **Communications** exercise. Doing it that way is an ice breaker. During the debriefing, be sure to honor those who liked the experience and those who didn't; both are OK. This lets people experience having their opinions respected. I point out that this exercise demonstrates that we can do more than one thing at a time— collect data, do a communication exercise, and get to know people in a new way.

Remember to own your own preferences about eye contact but not to impose them on the group. This can be especially important if you have a mixed racial or ethnic group that consists of some people who believe that looking straight in the eye is a mark of respect and some who believe that looking down is a mark of respect. Be careful not to impose one group's rules on everyone. A man said he liked the back-to-back part because leaning against someone else's back felt good and he couldn't get that close to a stranger if he were looking at him.

Move the "eye level" segment along quickly, and send people home to think about it. At the second meeting people often report that they have changed the way they talk with their children as a result of that exercise. One woman announced that since that role play she has put a chair at one side of her desk at work and now asks people to sit while she interviews them. She realized during the exercise that she was very uncomfortable looking up at people.

If someone objects to role playing, you can remind people that a role play like this "eye level" exercise is not meant to be a "real" interaction. Role playing is a way to symbolize, in a compressed time, an experience for the whole body, much as printed words symbolize experiences for the eyes and spoken words symbolize experiences for the ears. Role playing "reminds" our bodies, in a brief way, how we feel in real life situations.

4. I do the **Course Goals** very quickly. It honors people who like the big picture. Be sure that the questions comparing the goals of the course with the goals of the individuals are carefully answered. Whether or not you elaborate on content and methods is up to you. I prefer to spend the time demonstrating the methods with the Suggestion Circle or the Four Ways of Parenting. In case you get questions about process, absorb the material in "Who, Me, Lead a Group?" pages 5 to 9—How Adults Organize Learning Material and How Adults Take in Information.

5. The **Suggestion Circle** is a powerful way to share information and ideas quickly. Run the first one to get suggestions for yourself before you run one for someone else. Be sure people understand how the Suggestion Circle works: Get a contract from the focus person, the one receiving suggestions, to listen to all the suggestions offered. She can say "thank you," but that is all. If Mary says "Yes, but I tried four of those things, and I want to tell you why they didn't work," the reply is "Mary, you agreed to listen to the Suggestion Circle and think about the suggestions and make your own evaluation of them. If you would like more suggestions or the Four Ways of Parenting exercise about this problem at the next meeting, ask for them at goal-setting time." If a suggestion-giver wanders off into her own problem, ask her to concentrate on the focus person. If a receiver's thank-yous indicate approval or disapproval of the suggestions, ask her to keep her response nonjudgmental. I recommend that the Suggestion Circle be used at home when people want to collect ideas about unemotional issues. It could be misused if families send sharp hidden messages or critical messages about emotional issues. It could be subtly manipulated, outside of awareness, to fit a family's dysfunctional behavior.

6. Be sure to share your **Beliefs About Families.** You may want to add some of your own to the list. One of my beliefs is that people who come to a class have a right to know the value systems of the author and the teacher. Even if you look upon yourself as a true facilitator—"one who invites others to discover"—some people in the group may view you as an "authority." Sharing your values can reduce the time they spend wondering what your values are.

7. Many people say the **Four Ways of Parenting** is the single most helpful exercise in the entire course. I agree. Don't worry if people don't seem to understand it completely the first time;

stay in charge of it. Let them know that it will be part of every meeting. People often need a little practice before they use it freely. It is a good quick way to offer altenative parenting messages without having to choose the best way, or be an expert, or solve someone else's problem. Sometimes people come to a meeting five minutes early and use the exercise before class starts. One person can play all four parent roles if necessary.

The Four Ways of Parenting signs will be used at every meeting. They can be made of heavy paper attached to a long string and hung around the sender's neck. Some are done in letters and textures that suggest ideas. Jeanne Carsello's **Critical** sign is all sharp and pointy. Nancy O'Hara put cotton balls all over her **Marshmallow** sign; Judee Hansord's **Nurturing** sign is smooth and flowing. Betty Beach's **Structuring** sign is firm and has a bold border around the edge. Whatever way you have fun putting the textures and shapes together, put the word, very large, on the front and some descriptive words and phrases on the back.

FRONT	BACK
Nurturing	Offers unconditional love. Gives permission to do things well, to change, to succeed. "You are lovable and capable."
Structuring	Conveys ethics; sets limits; tells or shows how to do things well, to succeed. "You are capable; here is how."
Marshmallowing	Gives permission to fail, to stay stuck. "You are inadequate."
Criticizing	Tells or shows how to fail. "You are inferior."

8. This exercise, **High Self-Esteem Invitations,** is important because it introduces people to the way we will be working throughout the meetings. It says, "Here are some ways to look at your own behavior; here are some suggestions. Go home and observe your behavior, with love." It does not say, "Here is the *right* or the *new* or the *best* way to do it, and I expect you to change right now." The first approach assumes that people are doing a lot of things right, and that they will have a lot of strengths to share with each other. The positives for **Being** come under fire from people who have strong rules about needing to "earn" compliments or rules that strangers don't

know you well enough to be "sincere." Tell them to do the parts they are comfortable with. Sometimes the idea of using negatives (you did not do this thing well) as a self-esteem builder meets with cheers and people say "I agree, and I need to learn how to do that better!" On the other hand, I have had people in class who believe that you should only say positive things to children and completely ignore the negative. They say, "If you can't say something nice, don't say anything at all." I believe this idea is poison, and I say so. It is scary to think what would happen to us if nobody told us when we did something wrong. That is dangerous; so model how to say negatives in a healthy, growth-permitting way. Also, I learn something about myself each time I do this exercise, and that implies that we all can grow together.

Sometimes people tell me that they have never given **Beings** and think they should but can't because they feel "plastic" or "awkward." I assure them that it certainly feels this way for me when I am starting any new learning or skill, whether it is learning a foreign language, or playing tennis, or improving how I interact with others. I cannot perform new behaviors smoothly the first day, and I don't expect them to either. A feeling of discomfort is usual and will pass as they practice more. Maybe a feeling of discomfort is desirable. We can acquire empathy for people who are learning new skills—kids in school, adults on a new job, immigrants in a new culture, children and adults getting used to each other in a newly blended family. If people complain about the take-home exercise because they don't know the "right answers," reassure them that whatever they find out will be helpful. They may find out things about themselves that they like a lot.

It is important to **close** on time, so be sure to allow enough time for closing activities. If some people want to stay on and talk after closing time, that is their choice, but formal closing is the responsibility of the facilitator. You may be a prompt closer, but I have not always been. Since not closing on time discounts other people, I decided to be strict about it. My old casual habits were hard to change. I took an alarm clock to class, felt rather silly, and hoped people would not be offended. Instead, they cheered me on and complimented me when I stopped on time.

I think it is important to review assignments—it makes a nice wrap-up for the people who like that kind of order, and it takes only a few seconds.

Ending meetings with **Resentments and Appreciations** is a quick, open way to say "Everyone is important, and both negative and positive feedback are OK." I have received Appreciations that I

34

never expected. I have expressed Appreciations that I might have forgotten to share. And the Resentments I have found fascinating. In some classes, it is weeks before anyone dares to breathe one. In other groups someone will jump in hard with big accusations at the first meeting. Encourage people not to justify their Resentments. Don't make any promises to do anything about these Resentments and Appreciations except to listen. Don't defend; just listen! Sometimes there is a big Resentment that we share, which we can't do anything about at the time, but the sharing seems to reduce the tension about it. Don't expect personal appreciation—if you get lots of it after the first meeting, you may have been inviting it or signaling that you expect it. People are often more appreciative of you after trust has been established and they have become a cohesive group.

Remember that people learn from modeling. We are teaching about nurturing—so don't forget to take good care of yourself.

I appreciate your reading this letter, and I resent that I can't see you and listen to your responses to it right now. Have a wonderful first class!

Love,

Jean

P.S. These are the Facilitator Affirmation samples. One facilitator says: I will stay in a mutual respect position for the two hours I am teaching. I am a warm, open person. I am a competent, powerful, intuitive facilitator. I flow with the group and do my job. My job is to provide and lay out the tools. It is their responsibility to pick and choose and use. I offer protection and permission, and I am successful.

And another facilitator says: I do not have to know all the answers; people in the group have a lot of knowledge. These people are lucky to have me. I can support them as they look for alternatives. It is important to let people discover for themselves the way they want to behave.

MEETING 1

BEFORE MEETING 1

1. Read "Who, Me, Lead a Group?", pages 1-27; read the book *Self-Esteem: A Family Affair,* and read all the Meeting plans and the Letters to Marj in this book.
2. Study Meeting 1 plan.
3. Reread *Self-Esteem: A Family Affair,* Chapter one, Four Ways of Parenting description, and Four Ways of Parenting exercise on pages 267-270 of that book.
4. Read the first Letter to Marj, pages 29-35.
5. Collect the following **supplies:**
   felt pens
   paper for name tags
   tape for hanging posters
   tape or pins for name tags
   half sheets of paper for note taking.
6. Make the following **visual aids:**

POSTERS
- Meeting 1 Goals, Meeting 1, page 36
- Ground Rules, Meeting 1, page 37
- Interview Questions, Meeting 1, page 38
- High Self-Esteem Invitations, Meeting 1, page 44

SIGNS
- Four Ways of Parenting signs, Marj 1, pages 32-33

DUPLICATED HANDOUTS
- Course Goals, Content and Methods, Meeting 1, page 48
- Three Balloon, Meeting 1 page 50
- Homework. Meeting 1 page 52

OPENING *(10 Minutes)*

Bookkeeping
Collect fees; get names, addresses, phone numbers; sell or issue copies of *Self-Esteem: A Family Affair* to each person.

NAMES
Hand out name tags and felt pens.

Say: *Print your name on this tag. Please make it large enough for everyone to see. One thing we will do in this group is get to know each other.*

Assemble people in a circle.

Ask: *Will each of you say your name aloud?*

GOALS
Post **Meeting 1 Goals** poster.

MEETING 1 GOALS
1. Ground Rules
2. Names and Goals
3. Communications
4. Goals of *Self-Esteem: A Family Affair*
5. Suggestion Circle
6. Beliefs About Families
7. Four Ways of Parenting
8. High Self-Esteem

Point to poster and read:

1. **Ground Rules**—*We will adopt ground rules for the meetings.*
2. **Names and Goals**—*We will learn each other's names and hear what people are hoping to accomplish during the meetings.*
3. **Communications Exercise**—*We will do a couple of exercises to improve our communications skills.*
4. **Goals of Self-Esteem: A Family Affair**—*We will compare the goals of this course with individual goals and expectations.*
5. **Suggestion Circle**—*We will learn a way to share suggestions with each other very quickly.*
6. **Beliefs About Families**—*We will examine the beliefs about families on which this course is based and compare them with our own.*
7. **Four Ways of Parenting**—*This is an exercise that allows us to look at different ways of parenting and make our own decisions about what we like and want to do.*
8. **High Self-Esteem Invitation**—*We will identify three ways of inviting high self-esteem.*

1. GROUND RULES
(5 Minutes)

Point to the **Ground Rules** poster.

```
GROUND RULES
1. Everyone Participates
2. Right to Pass
3. All Opinions Are
   Honored
4. Leader Respects
   Others and Self
5. Confidentiality
```

Read and explain each ground rule.

Say: ***Everyone participates*** *in all of the exercises, at least mentally, and this includes the leader.*

Say: *Everybody has the **right to pass.** If any one of us does not wish to share, to discuss something or do something, she has the right to pass and this right will be honored.*

Say: ***All opinions are honored.*** *All of our beliefs, values, attitudes and opinions are correct for us today, because they reflect how we have made sense out of our experiences so far. We may change our opinions when we get new information or have new experiences.*

Say: **Leader will respect self and others.** I plan to stay in the position of respect for people, and I invite you to do the same. This means that we will experience each other as equal, competent, human beings, who have come together to explore new ideas and practice new behaviors. We can agree to disagree and hear each other without deciding that one person's beliefs are right and the other's are wrong. When we disagree, I will not put down your ideas and I will not change my own in order to be pleasing to you. If I should slip out of this position, I hope you will remind me.

Say: **Confidentiality.** After our meetings, I will not discuss individuals and their activities here in a way that could be considered gossip. I may talk about my experiences in general. It is important in this group to try out new ideas and alternative behaviors. We need the freedom to say and do things, think about them, and continue or discontinue them without having to worry about someone outside the group hearing.

Ask: Is everyone in the group willing to keep these ground rules?

Ask: Do you wish to add any additional ground rules?

Ask: Does anyone want to join me in staying in the mutual respect position?

2. NAMES AND GOALS FINDING
(20-30 Minutes)

Point to **Interview** poster and read the list of interview questions:

INTERVIEW
Name

Describe your children if you have children.

Where did you find out about these Self-Esteem meetings?

What do you hope to get out of the meetings?

What is something you enjoy doing or do well?

Ask: Is there another interview question the group would like to include?

Say: This is not only a way to get to know people, it is also a communication exercise. Will you find a person whom you do not know or someone you want to get to know in a new way? Interview this person while you sit back-to-back with her. Do not look at your partner. After the interview you will introduce her to the

38

group. We will discuss later what you learned about eye contact or lack of it. You will have ten minutes in which to conduct your interview. If, after a few minutes, you dislike the back-to-back experience, turn and do the rest of the interview facing each other. When you ask your partner what she hopes to get out of the meetings, ask about her wishes and find out what tools she wants for getting along better with other people and herself.

After ten minutes reassemble people in a circle.

Say: *I will record your goals and refer to them throughout the eight sessions.*

Ask: *Will each of you introduce the person you interviewed to the whole group? Include answers to all the interview questions and any other impressions or information you want to share. You may each have two or three minutes.*

Record individual goals and wishes for later use.

Say: *I will be responsible for presenting tools, and I invite you to be responsible for using the tools to meet your own needs.*

OPTIONAL:
Those of you who are interested in improving your communication skills can do

each exercise, think about the exercise, and use it to try new ways of communicating. Keep the parts that you think will help you. Some of you want better ways to deal with specific behavior problems. As we do each exercise, think about how you might use the skills involved to deal with those behavior problems.

---

3. COMMUNICATIONS EXERCISE (5 Minutes)

Say: *The reason the interview was conducted back-to-back was to practice verbal communication.*

Ask: *Did anyone dislike talking and listening while looking away? Anyone like it? What did you dislike or what did you like?*

Say: *There are many ways to use eyes during communication. We will do an "eye levels" communication exercise. Remember your right to pass. One person will ask: "Will you do something for me?" The other will answer: "No." We will do this three different ways. You can compare the ways and decide which you prefer.*

Demonstrate all three of the following positions with a participant:
   1. Stand up facing your interview partner; look her in the eye; ask "Will you do

something for me?" She answers "No."

2. Kneel, look up and look your partner in the eye, repeat the question. She answers "No."
3. Stand tall; partner bend knee or kneel; look her in the eye; repeat the question.
4. Reverse roles, and repeat all three.

Ask: *Will each of you find a partner and repeat the exercise demonstrated?*

Reassemble people in a circle after about two minutes.

Ask: *Did anyone feel more "powerful" in one position than in another? Which one?*

Ask: *Did anyone feel more "listened to" in one position than in another? Which one?*

Ask: *In any of the three positions did you feel more "mutual respect"?*

Say: *Think about which position you use most often when you speak to your family. Do you like the way you do it?*

Ask: *Will you observe your behavior between now and the next meeting to see how you make eye contact with family members while talking with them? Notice whether you really do it the way you thought you did.*

4. GOALS OF SELF-ESTEEM: A FAMILY AFFAIR *(5 Minutes)*

Hand out copies of the **Course Goals, Content and Methods,** page 48. Give people a couple of minutes to glance at the sheet. Compare course goals and goals of the individuals.

Ask: *Can you fit your personal goals with the goals listed on this sheet?*
EXAMPLE:
Some specific goals that people mentioned during the introductions that will be met during the course are the following:
● Learn new ways to communicate
● Meet new people
● Have time away from the children to focus on myself
● Learn about what children the ages of mine need

Ask: *Did you hear specific individual goals mentioned during the introductions that do not fit with the goals of these meetings?*
EXAMPLE:
If a woman came only to learn about child development, would she prefer to find a child development class?
EXAMPLE:
A person expecting therapy should be referred to a therapy group.

5. SUGGESTION CIRCLE[1] (5-10 Minutes)

Say: *One problem-solving tool that we will practice at each meeting is the **Suggestion Circle**. This is a way to offer alternatives to someone who wants suggestions about a specific problem. With the Suggestion Circle we share alternatives without putting down anyone's ideas. The Suggestion Circle stimulates thinking and encourages each of us to take responsibility for our own problems. You may have done "brainstorming" in which you offered lots of ideas before judging their worth. The Suggestion Circle is different from brainstorming. We collect each person's highest quality suggestion the first time around.*

Say: *This is the way we do the Suggestion Circle:*
1. *I state my problem.*
2. *I ask someone to list the suggestions for me, if I want a written list.*
3. *Each person thinks of her best suggestion.*
4. *We go quickly around the circle; each person either tells me a one-sentence suggestion or passes.*
5. *I listen to each suggestion and do not say anything except "Thank you." I do not say "That was a good answer" or "That was a poor one."*

6. *I consider the suggestions and use them in the way that fits for me.*

Do a Suggestion Circle. State one problem and listen to the Suggestion Circle. Thank the participant, but do not comment on any answer.

EXAMPLE:
My nine year old often misses the school bus. What should I do?
Suggestions:
Take him to school. School is important.
Let him walk if it is not too far.
Let him ride his bike if it is safe.
Let him stay at home and study all day, no TV.
Buy him an alarm clock and show him how to use it.
Ask him what he needs to get to school on time.

Say: *Any one of you can ask for a Suggestion Circle anytime you want. Does anyone want one right now?* (If someone wants one, get a clear statement from her that she is willing to listen to each idea and to respond only with "thank you," and then do the Suggestion Circle.)

6. BELIEFS ABOUT FAMILIES (5 Minutes)

Say: *Before we start to practice alternative ways of parenting, let us examine the* beliefs about families on which the meetings are based and compare them with your own.

Ask: *Will you turn to page vii in Self-Esteem: A Family Affair? Will you read the* **Beliefs** *to yourself? Will you star the one that is most important to you?*

Say: *This is your workbook so please write in your book.*

OPTIONAL:
Send this home if short of time.

Go through the following questions for each item on the list.

Ask: *Did someone star this statement? Are you willing to tell the group why you starred it? Do any of you have a belief you would like to add to the list? You may extend it at any time.*

7. FOUR WAYS OF PARENTING
(20-25 Minutes)

Say: *One of the goals of this series of meetings is to practice skills for taking care of ourselves and other people. The Four Ways of Parenting exercise demonstrates both positive and negative ways to care for others or ourselves. By listening to all four ways we can strengthen our own positive parenting skills.*

42

Display all **four parenting** signs.

Say: *Here are four possible ways of responding when someone says, "My six year old stole something from a store. What shall I do?"*

Hold up the **Nurturing** sign.

Say: *I'm sorry your child did that. I know that you can handle the situation.*

Hold up the **Structuring** sign.

Say: *Tell your child, "This belongs to the store owner, not to you. I will go with you to return it. Now!"*

Hold up the **Marshmallowing** sign.

Say: *Well, I suppose he learned to steal from watching TV. There isn't much you can do.*

Hold up the **Criticizing** sign.

Say: *You must be a terrible parent to have a child who steals from a store. Next thing you know, he will steal a car!*

Open your text to page 14.

Say: *Will you open your text to page 14? There is a description of each of the Four Ways of Parenting which you can study before our next meeting. I will tell you something about each style of parenting and you may jot notes in your book if you want to.*

Hold up the **Nurturing** sign.

Say: *Nurturing is positive. It is supportive and caring. A nurturing parent helps* children and grown-ups get needs met, invites growth, and offers to be helpful.

Hold up the **Structuring** sign.

Say: *Structuring is a positive response. It sets limits, protects, asserts, demands responsible behavior, teaches ethics, and it tells how to do things well, to change, to win.*

Hold up the **Marshmallowing** sign.

Say: *Marshmallowing is negative. It sounds supportive or nurturing but invites children and grown-ups to be dependent. It covers them with sweetness that sounds good but doesn't help them solve their problem. It gives permission to fail.*

Hold up the **Criticizing** sign.

Say: *Criticizing is negative. It gives information in a destructive way, suggests ways to act like a loser, and tells how to fail.*

Say: *We all need to be parented or nurtured or cared for in some ways throughout our lives. To become familiar with this exercise we will read aloud the example on page 15, "I'm going to read a book called Self-Esteem: A Family Affair, and I don't really know if I'll find it helpful."*

Place an empty chair in front of the group.

Say: *Will one of you sit on the chair and listen to the four responses to that statement and tell us which one is most*

helpful to you? You are the listening person.

Ask: *Will four people stand behind her, wear the signs designating your roles, and read the four different parenting messages from the book? You are the sending persons.*

Hand out the four parenting signs and get the sending people to stand behind the chair, out of sight of the listening person on the chair. If no one volunteers, play all four roles yourself.

Ask the listening person:
Will you read the situation on page 15 to the sending people and then close your book and listen? When she has finished reading . . .

Say to the sending people:
Now you may read your roles in any order. When they have finished reading . . .

Stand facing the person on the chair.

Ask: *Did you hear a message that was helpful to you? One that was not?*

Say: *Each of us can turn up or down the volume on what comes into our ears. You can pretend that you are a radio receiver with four knobs. You can turn up the volume and hear the helpful message louder. Do you want to do that?*

(If the listening person says yes, ask the person reading that message to read it again in the

43

same tone of voice as before. Ask the listening person to allow herself to hear it *louder.*)

Ask: *Do you want to soften a message that is not helpful?*

(If the listening person says yes, ask the sending person to say it again, and ask the listening person to turn the volume down *low.*)

Ask: *Is there some message you wish you had heard that you did not hear?*

(If the listening person says yes, find out what she wants to hear and ask one of the sending people to say it to her; or you step behind her, put on the appropriate sign, and say the message.)
At the close of the exercise, derole each role player.

Ask: *Will each of you who was reading in this situation take off your sign and be the competent, loving person you really are? Give up any negative feelings you may have had during the role play.*

Ask: *Will the group look at the people who played negative roles, give up any negative feelings they may have had toward these people, and see these people as the positive people they are?*

Take back the signs and thank all five, especially the listening person, for participating.

Ask: *Would someone else like to read one of the problems on page 16 or offer a situation of her own choice?*

44

(If yes, repeat the exercise.)

Say: *We will practice the Four Ways of Parenting at each meeting. People can bring in problems or choose situations from the book. Playing or listening to each of the four roles helps people hear what they are saying and sharpens their parenting skills.*

Put the four parenting signs away and move the empty chair back to its place.

8. HIGH SELF-ESTEEM INVITATION
(20 Minutes)

Point to **High Self-Esteem Invitations** three-balloon poster.

HIGH SELF-ESTEEM INVITATIONS

I LIKE YOU (For Being)

I LIKE WHAT YOU DO (For Doing)

YOU CAN DO BETTER (For Doing Poorly)

Ask: *Will you turn to page 272 in your book and read the definition of self-esteem?*

Say: *This is the definition of self-esteem that we will be using during these meetings: "Self-esteem is one's assessment of the extent to which one is lovable and capable." This includes believing that one is lovable and capable and acting in a lovable and capable way. Self-esteem is not to be confused with conceit or macho, which are cover-ups for lack of real self-esteem.*

Say: *We offer our children high self-esteem when we give them positive messages about what they do and who they are. This exercise offers us three ways to do that.*

Say: *Think if you prefer to hear an "I like you," a "You did well," or a "You didn't do that well enough; I expect more of you" invitation to high esteem.*

Ask: *Will all of the people who want an "I like you" or a reward for **Being** stand in one part of the room? Will all those who like rewards for **Doing well** stand in another part of the room, and all of those who want to hear the **Doing poorly** (Can-do-better) messages stand in a third area of the room?*

Go to the **Being** group.

Say: *A positive message for Being is a reward that is not earned. It is given just because the person exists. It says, "I like you, I'm glad you are alive." It might be calling a person by the name she wants to be called or asking, "How are you?"*

Give a positive **Being** message to each individual.
EXAMPLE:
Shake hands. "I'm glad you are here." "Hello." "I look forward to knowing you." Or read examples in the text, page 17.

Go to the **Doing well** group.

Say: *A reward for Doing Well is earned by the person. It invites her to have high self-esteem because of what she has accomplished. It says, "You did a good job. I like the way you did that. I see you are improving in the way you do that."*

Give a reward for **Doing well** to each person in the group.
EXAMPLE:
"Thank you for being on time." "You have good posture." "I liked the way you interviewed your partner." "Thank you for standing in this group." Or choose examples from *Self-Esteem: A Family Affair*, page 18.

Go to the **Can-do-better** group.

Say: *A high self-esteem message can be given for something a person did poorly. It offers alternatives or gives structure and security. A quiet "Stop* that!" indicates "You are capable." A screamed "How could you do a thing like that?" indicates "You are not capable." Messages about negative behavior can build self-esteem and give security when they are given in a way that honors the worth and competence of the person to whom they are given. One way to do this is to use three messages: (1) Don't do this . . . (2) because . . . (3) do this instead. Or, (1) Don't do this . . . (2) because . . . (3) you can think of a better way to do it. EXAMPLE:

(1) "Don't run with the scissors. (2) You might get hurt. (3) Walk when you have scisssors in your hand." Virginia Satir talks about the importance of learning to "give criticism as a gift."[2] The person receiving the criticism will not necessarily enjoy the criticism but can choose to hear and benefit from it.

Give a **Can-do-better** high esteem message to each person in the group for doing something poorly. (If there is no one standing there, pretend there is someone there and give the message.)

Say: *I will give you a Can-do-better message about being late. "Don't be late for things that are important to you. Lateness can be self-damaging behavior. You can decide when it is important to be on time and be there!"*

Reassemble people in a circle.

Say: *Look at pages 17, 18, and 19 in your text. Here are examples of the three types of messages. Please study these pages before the next meeting.*

Hand out a **Three Ballon** sheet to each person.

Say: *Here is a sheet on which you may record the messages you are offering to someone.*

Ask: *Will each of you think of a person you want to invite to have high self-esteem? Write the name of that person on the sheet. Also write a specific day and a time like ten or fifteen minutes in which you will record the messages you offer this person. You may write in the words that you use or make marks in each balloon to indicate the number of times you give that specific kind of message. If you give a message that is hard to classify like "Pass the salt," you can record it where you think it goes or you can write it in the blank space and ask the group how they would classify it at the next meeting.*

Show a sample sheet, your own or the example included here, page 51.

Say: *You don't have to do anything different; just count what you usually say. If it seems silly or stilted to count, you can do it anyway—to collect accurate data on how you are sending* messages. You need not show the results to anyone else.

CLOSING *(5 Minutes)*

Take care of any business details that have not been completed such as time and place of next meeting, or collecting fees.

Say: *If you have to come late or miss a meeting, please find a way to catch up without disturbing the group.*

Point to the **Goals** poster and briefly note the content covered. Review the homework for the next class:

1. *If you like eye contact, observe how often you use eye contact with your family while you are talking and listening to them.*
2. *Think about beliefs.*
3. *Record your messages on the Three Ballon sheet.*
4. *Read Preface, Chapters one and two in the text; study pages 14, 17, 18, and 19 especially; note pages 256 and 257; and skip pages 20-27 (Plastics through Good Mother). We will do these later. Bring your book to the meetings.*

RESENTMENTS AND APPRECIATIONS
(5 Minutes)

Say: *It is important to end each class with Resentments and Appreciations. This lets us leave our Resentments here in the group where we may be able to do something about them, rather than complaining to someone outside the group who is not able to do anything about them. Any Resentments are OK to say. All are to be listened to but not answered. Take responsibility for your own feelings and behavior. Say, "I resent that we allowed so many interruptions," rather than "I resent that Jane is so long-winded."*
EXAMPLES:
"I resent that I was tired."
"I resent being hot."

Say: *If you have some Appreciations for other people or for yourself, will you please say them now? It is important to end each class with Appreciations. This lets us collect good feelings as we leave the group, and it gives us practice saying positive things to each other.*
EXAMPLES:
"I appreciate that you all came."
"I appreciate the pleasant room we have to meet in."
"I appreciate the high level of energy that you maintained during the class."
"I appreciate the way in which you shared."
"I appreciate that someone took right of passage."

Say: *Thank you. This meeting is over. I will see you next week.*

Course Goals, Content, and Methods

GOALS

To give support to the people in the group.

To give and get positive reinforcement and teach others how to do the same.

To work with the people in the room. This is not a group to "fix" children or "change" spouses but to help those who are here learn to take better care of children, themselves, and other adults.

To focus on the needs of the people in this group as growing human beings and on the emotional, developmental needs of children.

To practice tools everyone can use rather than repeatedly focusing on one person's problems.

To be a growth and sharing group, not a therapy group. This means to work on here-and-now problem solving, to invite people to look at alternative ways of initiating and responding to communications and not to analyze people's early experiences.

To have fun.

CONTENT

The ideas and tools for building self-esteem that will be developed are Affirmations, Responsibility, Development of the Three Parts of the Personality, Stroke Theory, and Discounts.

Each will be explained and the thread of each can be traced throughout the meetings.

These tools are based on Transactional Analysis, a psychological system originally developed by Dr. Eric Berne that explains human behavior and offers workable methods for motivation and change.[3]

METHODS

Learnings will be presented in a variety of ways. Experiences will be connected with theories. Each learning will be offered visually (to the eyes), auditorily (to the ears), and kinesthetically (to the body) to accommodate different learning styles.

There are over forty separate opportunities to consider information or practice using communication skills. Class members can participate in as many as they like. They can use each of the learnings for their own problems if they choose. Since most real learnings take place between meetings—during the time people consider, try things out, modify, incorporate or discard ideas—these meetings will not be compacted into a weekend. Class members can reinforce their learnings by reading,[4] by listening to tapes, and by practicing the role plays.

Three Balloon

Name_____ Date_____ Time_____

Three Balloon

Name **Annette Bodnes** Date **May 2** Time **7:30-7:40 A.M.**

Homework

1. Observe eye contact.
2. Think about Beliefs (or Assumptions) page vii in text.
3. Fill in Three Balloon sheet.
4. Read Preface, Chapters one and two (skip pages 22-27), pages 14, 17, 18, 19, 256, and 257.

Notes

1. Thanks to Otho Hesterly for introducing the author to the "Give Me Your Ideas Exercise," here called the Suggestion Circle.
2. Virginia Satir, *Peoplemaking* (Palo Alto, Calif.: Science and Behavior Books, 1972).
3. Eric Berne, *TA in Psychotherapy* (New York: Grove Press, 1961).
4. Jean Illsley Clarke, *Self-Esteem: A Family Affair* (Minneapolis: Winston Press, 1979).

LETTER TO MARJ 2

Dear Marj,

Spending last weekend with you was delightful! I like your kids and the easy way you all play together and work together, and yet you all seem to come and go and pursue your own interests. You have a lot of wisdom and fun to share with other people, and I'm happy that I am one of those people.

About the second meeting—

Do the **Opening** on time whether all people are in place or not. Waiting signals people that it is not important to be on time. Remember that you set the tone for the meeting in the way you greet people during the first three minutes. All people need positive strokes, and this name tag exercise gives a positive stroke to each person. Be sure to get yours. This is the meeting at which **Affirmations** and **Parenting Tips** start. Bruce Pederson uses permanent name tags which he introduces at this meeting. Bruce gives each person a firm four by six inch card and asks him to put on it his name and to represent each of his children: a red dot for an infant, an orange dot for a six to eighteen month old, a yellow dot for an eighteen month to three year old, a green dot for each three to six year old, a light blue dot for each six to twelve year old, a dark blue dot for each thirteen to nineteen year old. These colors correspond to the colors of the **affirmation cymbals** and **posters**. As Bruce introduces each new set of affirmations, he can see at a glance who has children in each developmental stage.

Do the interviews quickly. This honors the new person, but it does not discount the people who attended the first meeting. Invite new people to find out about the first meeting by talking with another class member during the week. This is the last meeting at which I accept new members. People who want to start on the third meeting have missed one fourth of the course, and that's too much.

Here are those important **Ground Rules** again. They offer protection. When we are considering a topic as close to our core as how well we parent children, we all need protection. If your group added Ground Rules such as "Start and Stop on Time" or "Say it as it is," be sure those are on the poster.

Posting the **Goals** is reassuring to people who enjoy structure and who like to learn visually. If people are not interested in the parenting tips, drop goal six. It is important to invite people to add goals or needs at every meeting. If you can't meet a goal, say so.

Sometimes a topic will be addressed in an exercise in a later meeting. If so, ask the person if he is willing to wait. Often a topic can be addressed from the experience in the group. "Do any of you know of resources Kent can draw on for help with his situation?"

I sometimes reorder exercises. I switch the order of the Affirmations and the Parenting Tips in response to people's requests. Or I offer Modes of Discounting before the seventh meeting. I infrequently switch the order of the Responsibility exercises because they have been arranged by long trial and error and seem to build well the way they are. I do not vary the order of the Stroke exercises. That is the one thread in which each exercise is dependent upon the previous ones. They are carefully arranged to allow people to explore their own stroke myths with maximum protection and invitation to accept themselves as worthwhile persons and to grow.

If someone wants a **Suggestion Circle**, I usually do it as soon as I finish with the **Goals** poster. If someone wants a **Four Ways of Parenting** exercise (abbreviated as Four Parent) in this meeting, I urge them to wait until we do the Four Parent skills exercise. During later meetings I often do a Four Parent before anything else—even before name tags, if someone comes early and wants help.

1. Sometimes people will have done a lot of thinking about the **Beliefs** and will want to talk about them. This may be an important part of their own value-examination journey. Other groups skip through this quickly.

   Be rigid about following the rules for the Suggestion Circle (Meeting 1, page 41). Do not allow people to say "Yes, but," or "Don't you think," or "If only." You can speed the action by standing in front of each person as he offers his suggestion. After the last suggestion, ask the person with the problem to report back on his decision at the next meeting if he wants to.

   If someone says in response to the Things to Do Instead of Hitting, "Yes, but when I get that mad I don't think," ask him to do the A to Z exercise—it's a start toward optional behavior.

2. **Good Mothers and Good Fathers** is an important exercise. Move it *fast* so you get *old messages* instead of thoughtful judgments. Be sure to include your own. You can give permission to list both positive and negative messages by offering one of each, for example: "Don't praise your children because they might get a big head," and "Love kids." Urge people not to be judgmental about these—just to write them down quickly. I find that the toughest people to get early messages from are professionals—psychologists, ministers, teachers. Their lists often contain items like: "is concerned about the child's positive self-esteem; provides adequate

56

religious education." This is not "early" talk. Go for kid words. Say, "If you didn't talk like that when you were six or seven, don't write it down."

Combine the messages that are handed in and duplicate them for the next meeting. Number the items on the list so you can assign it by sections. If the list is short, add some messages from the examples in *Self-Esteem: A Family Affair*, pages 24-27, and be sure to tell people you did that.

3. Nancy O'Hara designed the **Four Ways of Parenting** exercise "because," she said, "I believe it is a very powerful exercise, and its full impact is often not grasped by participants." She developed this nifty way to familiarize people with the four roles in the hope that more people will ask for a Four Parent exercise whenever they want one. Make sure the words on the cards are visible from several feet away. If people disagree about where the cards go, this is OK—people hear things differently. Remember to take cards yourself.

Do this Four Ways of Parenting exercise quickly—about ten minutes on the teaching exercise and ten minutes on the role play. Play all the roles yourself if no one volunteers. Encourage people not to worry if the differences among the four ways don't seem completely clear. Often people do not become fluent in doing this exercise until the fourth or fifth meeting. Honor people's right to pass.

4. "Your Eggs Are Getting Cold," the mother said. "So?" the child replied. "You don't pay any attention to me," the mother complained. "I do. I just asked you a question," the child insisted.

While people rewrite the items on the Your Eggs Are Getting Cold list they often groan and laugh a lot. The sharing in the groups of three or four is important because it gives people a chance to hear different interpretations of the same item. (See pages 81-82.) "There are no clean socks in my drawer" was a particularly difficult one for my group to rewrite. We tried "I need some clean socks," and "I have no socks left," and "I'm out of socks again," all of which are more examples of making a statement that does not indicate who is **responsible.** Finally we got "Have you washed my socks?" and "Are you planning to wash my socks today?" both of which are direct questions. Sometimes people say, "Yes, but everybody at my house knows what this means, so what's wrong with it? Why should I change?" Well, everyone has the right to pass. Nobody has to change. These exercises are offered to give people options. As far as this skill of replacing indirect questions with direct ones is concerned, many of the people that I know who have tried it have liked it.

5. **Affirmations** are exciting to do. If you run short of time, compress somewhere else, but don't neglect affirmations.

When you do the exercise in which people receive and feel a **Being** and then a **Doing**, listen to your own demonstration examples and to the group's to be sure that people don't add a Doing to the Being. "I like you," not "I like you because . . ." I think that "I like your smile," is a Doing. "Will you still like me on a day when I have no smiles?" I ask the group where in their bodies they feel the Beings and Doings to show that people experience those feelings in different places and to give them permission to experience these bodily feelings.

I use **affirmation cymbals.** They are circles two inches in diameter, with the affirmations printed on them. I use red for the birth to six months set, orange for six to eighteen months, yellow for eighteen months to three years, green for three years to six years, a light blue for six to twelve years, and dark blue for thirteen to nineteen years. I order laminated affirmation cymbals and blocks and posters from Affirmation Enterprises, Post Office Box 21, Savage, Minnesota 55378. You can do that, or make your own, or encourage people to make their own. Whatever you do, find ways for kinesthetic persons to have affirmations to write or touch as well as to read and hear. Some of the facilitators use **affirmation blocks** and report that men like them especially well. When I first started exploring how the afffirmations could be adapted for use with parents, it was not intuitively clear to me how to do that. I realized that the affirmations are powerful and important, but I floundered for some months before I evolved clear ways to offer them and easy ways to apply them. I delved into each affirmation and found other ways of expressing it without changing the meaning. "You have every right to be here" became "I have the right to exist." "Your needs are OK with me" became "I have the right to have needs and to have them met." Then I considered the difference between needs and wants. Needs keep me alive and help me to move through my current developmental stage. Wants are wishes that allow me to avoid my tasks or to do them in the way that I want to. I "need" stimulation from other people. I "want" to travel to China. Teenagers "need" social interaction with people of all ages and especially with people their own age. They may "want" to have that interaction by driving a certain car to a specific party.

"I'm glad you are the sex you are" became "Persons of both sexes have the right to be full persons, and each individual has the right to enjoy being the sex he or she is and to have that sex be accorded full respect." "You don't have to hurry and grow up" became "My daughter has the right to develop on her own time.

She does not have to grow up fast to please me, and she does not have to stay little in order not to threaten me." "I like to hold you" became "Each of us has the right to feel lovable, and I will remember that people need love most when they are behaving in ways that make them seem least lovable."

When I first present the affirmations, some people say, "Wow, these are great!" Other people say, "These sound phony." I remember that there are reasons why people respond as they do and that I do not need to understand the reasons. It is my job to offer options, theirs to evaluate. I think of facetious ways to offer the messages. Sometimes I can reach people by being absurd. "Which of these affirmations do you want to see in skywriting?" "How about on a batik T-shirt?" "I have those needlepointed in earth tones on the backs of my dining room chairs, and our dinner parties are much more fun since I did that." (That's not really true, but it is such a good idea I think I will do it!) "How about making posters of each one of those for a long hallway or having the kids make them," or . . . whatever.

If I am short of time I ask the group to choose which of the three age groups to read Beings to. Or I skip the three readings, turn to the worksheets, page 49 in text, and ask them to get in groups of three and share what they plan to do.

People who have the permission and the skills to accept affirmations for themselves will enjoy hearing them. People who do not have permission to ask for what they need and want, or people who have a rule in their heads that anything you ask for is no good may resist using affirmations for themselves. Honor that. They may get some permission to reconsider those rules when you explore Stroke Rules in Meetings 3 and 4.

6. **Parenting Tips** are taken from the material referred to in the bibliography and from a lifetime of reading and teaching. The information also reflects my personal experience of living with three children and their friends. The tips are offered not as a recipe for raising children but as a composite of the best information, ideas, and experiences of the participants in the parenting groups where the tips were tested and revised. You can challenge them and add to them. You can invite people to examine them, think about them, try them on, enjoy them, improve upon them, and use them to increase their own and their children's happiness.

When you do **Parenting the Birth to Six-Month-Old Infant** section, you might like to give reference readings. You probably have lots of good ones. If I give only one, I give *Raising OK Kids*, by Babcock and Keepers, because it best points out that the job of the parent includes getting the parent's own needs met. Anything you can do to reinforce good care for the infant and the parent during this period is important. Sometimes mothers need permission to go ahead and give full care. They can remember that these particular demands will last for only a few months.

7. Now you get to start the formal teaching about **Strokes!** And what a variety of beliefs about strokes there are: "Children need strokes—adults don't. Some people don't need any. I never get any. I don't need any." This is why the Interaction exercise is used to introduce strokes. It cuts through the "I never-give-or-get-any" myths and it also lays to rest the idea that all strokes feel good. This exercise, combined with information about marasmus, generally cuts out long sessions of "Yes, but are you sure strokes are really important?" "Don't you think somebody just made this up?", or "Isn't stroking manipulative?" If I get questions like that, I refer back to this exercise and remind people that since we all give strokes every day we had better be giving the kinds we want to give.

You probably have specific information about marasmus, and you may know good references to give people who want to know more about it. Here is what I know: Marasmus is the name given by John Bowlby to identify the wasting away of infants as a result of an inadequate amount of loving attention.[1] Touching the skin of an infant stimulates growth, both physical and intellectual growth. Sometimes parents with a great big "Don't touch" message feel more comfortable about touching their children when they know it helps the kids to be smarter.

Interaction is the most important exercise of the day. It sets the foundation for all the work on stroking. Be sure to build protection into this exercise by reminding people of the right to pass on the whole exercise or any part of it. Sometimes people don't want to give the negatives because they are feeling so good from the positives. This is OK. Someone suggested giving the negatives first. I decided against this. I don't care if they skip the negatives, but I don't want to risk having people getting hooked on some negatives and then not feeling the positives.

Debriefing (deroling) is very important. I knew one person who held negative feelings from this exercise for weeks. I had not been careful enough to stress getting out of the role play and back into the here and now. I am glad she finally told me about it, for then I could and did invite her to let the bad feelings go. I will remember that it is always important to derole after a role play.

Recording the most- and least-liked items usually gives me a lot of data. The same item, perhaps the hug, may be both a least- and a most-liked. One woman says, "Women are only supposed to hug men." The woman next to her says, "Oh no, women are only allowed to hug women." Sometimes a hug is used to avoid eye contact or talking. If you have both men and women in the group, you may find their responses quite different. Generally men in our culture feel freer to push physically than women do. Sometimes a woman will say, "I liked the push away the best! I've wanted to do that for a long time!" Stay nonjudgmental! Sometimes people who believe that all communications should be "sincere" are upset with the role play. Invite them to remember that people learn in many ways and that most people learn best when they hear, see, and do. *Anyone has the right to pass on any exercise.* You could add more columns to this exercise if you want to, such as "Strokes I wish I gave most often."

8. Concerning the **Five Kinds of Strokes** exercise: If I am short of time I skip the marble exercise. However, an advantage of this exercise is that it does move the learning from a visual to a kinesthetic experience. Some of us respond differently to symbols we feel in our hands than to symbols we see on paper. Many people associate marbles with childhood, and some of us become aware of our wishes about our behavior more easily when we are holding marbles than when we are looking at a paper. This is an open-ended exercise to start people thinking. It is not intended to end with "right answers." If you can't find red, blue, and green marbles you can use candies. Avoid reinforcing racism by using white for positive strokes and black for negative ones. Jean Koski added the marbles to this exercise. She uses them all through the meetings by setting out three little bowls of marbles on a Three Balloon Sheet before each meeting. She believes that this encourages people to think about what they said and did so far that day.

Jean discovered that she had been counting the negatives and not counting (discounting) the positives she gave her children. The marbles helped her realize ways in which she is a good Mom.

If no one wants to give examples, there are other ways to review the Five Kinds of Strokes. Sometimes I give three people positives for **Being,** three people positives for **Doing,** three people negatives for **Doing poorly,** and I ask them to give me three examples of **Plastics** and three examples of **Don't be's.** You might categorize the positive words they put on each other's name tags. Or invite people to add items to the examples on pages 18, 19, and 20 in *Self-Esteem: A Family Affair.*

Do some planning about time. In case your group does a lot of Suggestion Circles and you have to compress material, think about what you will compress and/or what you can send home. Do not omit the Four Ways of Parenting. Do not fail to honor all homework the following week.

Stop the other activities early enough so the **Closing** is not rushed. I made the closing Affirmation poster round with lots of colors and bold printing. Don't forget **Resentments** and **Appreciations.** Listen. Do not respond or defend. I *resent* that I can't check out each of these exercises with you in person, but I *appreciate* your correspondence. Have a wonderful second class! I think those folks are lucky to have you!
Love,

Jean

MEETING 2

1. Study Meeting 2 plan.
2. Be thoroughly familiar with Preface, Chapters one and two and pages 256 and 257 in *Self-Esteem: A Family Affair.*
3. Read the second Letter to Marj.
4. Reread "Who, Me, Lead a Group?", Question 2, Step 1 and Question 5.
5. Collect the following **supplies:**
   paper for name tags
   felt tip pens
   masking tape or pins
   whole sheets of paper
   half sheets of paper
   marbles—red, green, blue
   chalk board or large newsprint
6. Make the following **visual aids:**
POSTERS
- Ground Rules, Meeting 1, page 37
- Meeting 2 Goals, Meeting 2, page 64
- All six Affirmation Posters, Meeting 2, page 70; 3, page 101; 4, page 123; 5, page 151; 6, page 172; 7, page 199
- Closing Affirmation Poster Meeting 2, page 78

SIGNS
- Four Ways of Parenting signs
- Affirmation cymbals for Being, Marj 2, page 70

CARDS
- White and colored cards for Four Ways of Parenting exercise, pages 79-80

DUPLICATED HANDOUTS
- Class roster
- Interaction sheet page 83

- Your Eggs Are Getting Cold page 81
- Homework, Meeting 2, page 85

OPENING (5-10 Minutes)

Post the posters
NAMES
Hand out name tags and felt pens as people come in.

Ask: *Will you work in pairs, and choose a person different from last week's partner? Print your partner's name and something positive about him on the name tag.*

Ask: *Will you introduce your partner and tell the group the positive thing you wrote about your partner?*

OPTIONAL:
If there are any new persons, interview them for the information that was obtained from the others at the first meeting—how many children, their ages, why the person is attending, what the person hopes to get out of this group, and one thing this person does for fun. Ask each person who was at first meeting to tell one thing we did at the first meeting.

GROUND RULES

Point to the **Ground Rules** poster.

Ask: *Will someone who remembers a ground rule state it?*
EXAMPLE
1. Everyone participates.
2. Everyone has the right to pass.
3. All opinions are honored.
4. Leader respects others and self.
5. Group will practice confidentiality.
6. Any other ground rules the group may have added.

GOALS

Point to **Meeting 2 Goals** poster.

MEETING 2 GOALS
1. Beliefs
2. Good Mothers and Good Fathers
3. Four Ways of Parenting
4. Responsibility
5. Affirmations for Being and Recycling
6. Parenting Tips
7. What Are Strokes?
8. Five Kinds of Strokes
9. Additions
10. Celebrations

Read the goals and negotiate.
1. *Beliefs—We will explore more thoughts about the beliefs on which Self-Esteem: A Family Affair meetings are based.*

2. *Good Mothers and Good Fathers—We will collect early messages that people have in their heads about what good mothers and good fathers do.*
3. *Four Ways of Parenting—We will practice and compare.*
4. *Responsibility—We will practice a communications exercise on being responsible for asking for what we want. It is called Your Eggs Are Getting Cold.*
5. *Affirmations for Being—We will identify them, practice listening to them for ourselves, and think of ways to offer them to other people. Recycling—We will explain the theory and give some examples.*
6. *Parenting Tips—Does anyone want time to explore Parenting Tips on infants birth to six months old?*
7. *What are Strokes?—We will define the word "stroke."*
8. *Five Kinds of Strokes—We will identify, experience, and compare different kinds of strokes.*
9. *Additions—Does anyone have suggestions for topics to be addressed by a Suggestion Circle or a Four Parent?*
10. *Celebrations—Does anyone want to share a celebration or an awareness from the past week? (Do this now.)*

1. BELIEFS *(5-10 Minutes)*

Ask: *Will you turn to page vii (in the first edition or v in the second) in your book and*

64

share any further thought you have had about Beliefs?

Say: *Another Belief might read "If the mother's and father's needs are met, the children's needs will be met and child abuse will be prevented."*

Ask: *How many of you agree with this statement? How many disagree?*

Lead a Suggestion Circle on things adults can do instead of hitting children. (See Directions for Suggestion Circle, Meeting 1, page 41.)

Ask: *Will anyone who is interested in identifying Things to Do Instead of Hitting make an A to Z list and bring it to the next meeting? Letter from A to Z on a paper. After each letter write one way to drain off anger and let it go without hurting another person or yourself. Include at least one way to resolve a problem that leads to anger. The list that Colleen Shaskin wrote, page 145 in your textbook, is an example.*

2. GOOD MOTHERS AND GOOD FATHERS *(5-10 Minutes)*

Say: *The purpose of this exercise is to list old ideas or early messages that we have received about parenting. We will update them next week. "Old" means "When I was*

little, I got the idea that this is what good moms and good dads did." I may or may not agree with those ideas now.*

Pass out half sheets of paper.

Ask: *Will you spend about three minutes listing the earliest messages that you remember hearing (or knowing without being told) about what a "good mother is and does" if you are a woman or what a "good father is and does" if you are a man? Write quickly. Jot down whatever comes into your head. Use six year old's words like "bakes cookies," "loves her kids," "works long hours," or "scolds a lot." Don't worry about being right or wrong. Try to remember messages from when you were little. Some of the items may contradict each other, and you may not believe these things now. Remember that you don't have to share your list if you don't want to.*

Collect lists

Say: *If you are willing to hand in your lists without your names on them, I will duplicate them for discussion at the next meeting.*

3. FOUR WAYS OF PARENTING[2] *(20 Minutes)*

Say: *At the last meeting we did a Four Ways of Parenting exercise. Our homework assignment was to study page 14 in* Self-Esteem: A Family Affair. *Before we do a Four Parent, we will review some of the words or phrases that can be used to describe each of the four ways of parenting. We will give some examples of what each of the four kinds of parents might say or do. Make notes on page 14 if you want to.*

Lay out the **Four Ways of Parenting signs** in the middle of the floor. Distribute the **white cards** with descriptive *words* to the group members.

Ask: *Will each of you read your cards out loud and place them near the sign they describe? If you aren't sure, ask the group to help you.*

Distribute the **colored cards** with examples of *messages* to the group members.

Ask: *Will each of you read your cards aloud and ask the group which sign to place them by?*

Say: *I hope this exercise helped you get a clearer picture of how the Four Ways of Parenting exercise is designed.*

Ask: *Any further questions? Remember, this is a structure to help people to think and decide about their own parenting. It is not meant to tell you "the only right ways" to be nurturing and structuring, but to help you think about how you want to do that.*

Pick up the signs; leave the cards on the floor for people to look at during the Four Ways of Parenting exercise. Pick a topic that was mentioned during goal setting, or ask if someone has one they want to hear right now, or choose one from page 16 or 46-47 in the text. Lead the Four Ways of Parenting exercise.

Set out a chair for the listening person.

Hand out **Four Ways of Parenting** signs.

Ask the listening person: *Will you listen to all four messages without answering?*

Say to the sending people: *You may play the four roles in any order.*

When they have finished ask the listening person: *Were there some messages that were especially helpful for you? Is there a message that you want changed or added?*

If so, find out what and give the message. Get ideas from the whole group.

Ask: *Will you think of yourself as a radio with four stations? You can turn the volume up or down on any station. Are there any messages that you want to have repeated so you can practice hearing them more loudly or more softly?*

If so, have them repeated exactly as they were said the first time.

Ask: *Did you change the volume? Will each of you appreciate*

66

your own willingness and ability to role play different ways of parenting?

Will you take off your sign and separate yourself from the role you were playing, which may have been very different from the way you really are?

Will everyone in the group see these five persons as they really are?

Collect the signs.

4. RESPONSIBILITY
(10-15 Minutes)

Say: *We will be doing a series of exercises on responsibility. Each will be related to the affirmations and the developmental tasks addressed in that meeting. Encouraging responsible behavior that is appropriate to each age level helps children move from dependence to independence. Each exercise explores a different way in which we invite children and ourselves to be either clear or confused about responsibility. The first exercise is called* **Your Eggs Are Getting Cold.** *It focuses on communications that imply that someone has a desire or a responsibility without directly indicating who. It is important for children of all ages to know specifically who wants what and what is expected of them.*

Hand out copies of **Your Eggs Are Getting Cold** worksheets to each person.[3]

Say: *Each item is an example of an unquestion or secret demand that implies responsibility without being clear about who is responsible for what.*

Read aloud the examples.

Ask: *Will you rewrite the rest of the items on the list to ask a clear question or to make a clear demand in a way that assigns responsibility to someone? If you think of other examples, add these to the list.*

Say: *If you want to check out your revisions, you can apply the "So?" test. If "So?" is a logical response, write again. "I need a ride to school." "So?" "We have basketball practice at 4:30." "So?" "The coach said to be on time." "So?" "Will you please drive me to school?" "No, I can't leave now, but I am willing to let your sister drive you. Ask her."*

OPTIONAL:
If short of time, divide the class into groups, giving each group three or four items to work on.

Say: *After you have rewritten the items, move into groups of three or four and tell each other how you rewrote the items.*

Reassemble people in one circle.

Ask: *Will someone who rewrote item four read your changes for the group?*

Repeat for all times.

> *Will any of you who added other examples of unrequests, unquestions, or undemands read them to the group?*

Say: *Between now and our next meeting, notice whether you use unquestions, and if so, think of ways to ask your questions directly. "Will you" is a more direct way of asking a question than "could you" or "would you." "Do it now" is a clearer way to encourage responsibility than "I want you to." Remember that we encourage responsibility in children when we ask clear questions and encourage them to do the same.*

5. AFFIRMATIONS FOR BEING AND RECYCLING
(20-30 Minutes)

Say: ***Affirmations*** *and* ***negations*** *are two powerful kinds of communications. Affirmations are powerful positive messages that we give to each other and to ourselves that define who we are and how we expect to be treated. Whenever we interpret positively (verbally or nonverbally) the behavior or personal attributes of ourselves or others, we are giving affirmations. These are invitations to high self-esteem. Negations are powerful negative messages or interpretations that invite lower self-esteem.*

Say: *Affirmations or negations can be heard in three ways: from oneself, directly from someone else, or overheard.*

Ask: *Will you say out loud, all together, "I like myself"?*
Say it.

Ask: *Will you say to the person next to you, "I like you"?*
Say it.

Ask: *Will you say to another person that you like the person next to you?*
Say it.

Ask: *For how many of you is an affirmation most powerful if you give it to yourself? For how many of you is an affirmation most powerful if you hear it said to you by someone else? For how many of you is an affirmation most powerful if you hear someone say it to someone else about you in your hearing?*

Say: *This week, think of the way in which you most frequently communicate affirmations.*

Say: *Children who are older than six months need both positive Being and Doing messages in order to develop* high esteem. The next exercise gives us a chance to think about how we feel about these messages and to get some new insight into what we are offering other people. In this exercise we will work in pairs. One person will give a Being and then a Doing message to the other person. That person will listen, think about how he feels—what his actual body feelings are—but he will not give a verbal response. Then we will reverse roles.

Demonstrate with someone.
EXAMPLE:
"Hi, I'm glad I know you" (Being) and "Thanks for making the effort to get here today." (Doing)

Ask: *Will you find a partner and do this exchange now?*

After about three minutes reassemble the group.

Ask: *How many of you liked the two messages exactly the same?* (Ask for a show of hands.) *How many of you preferred the Being? Put your hand on your body where you felt the Being. How many of you preferred the Doing? Put your hand on your body where you felt the Doing. How many of you did not like one of the messages? How many of you think you prefer different ones on different days?*

Say: *Those of you who liked*

Beings better consider whether you give more Beings than Doings to other people.

Say: *If we give an ample amount of both to children, they can choose the ones they need that day.*

Say: *In her book* Becoming the Way We Are,[4] *Pam Levin Landheer lists affirmations that children need to hear during each developmental stage and again when they are grown-ups, recycling each stage in a more sophisticated form. These affirmations are organized into six sets, one for each stage.*

Point to the six **Affirmation** Posters: **Being, Doing, Thinking, Structure, Identity and Power,** and **Separation and Sexuality.**

Say: *We will explore a different set of affirmations at each meeting: how we communicate them, how we receive them, and how we can use them to help improve our own behavior.*

Point to the six **Affirmation** posters and single out the **Affirmations for Being** poster.

Say: *These six sets are the Affirmations for Growth. Today we will focus on the Affirmations for Being. They are particularly important for infants, for teenagers, for people who are ill, tired, hurt or vulnerable. They are important for everyone.*

Read the **Affirmations for Being** poster.

AFFIRMATIONS FOR BEING

You have every right to be here.
Your needs are OK with me.
You don't have to hurry (and grow up).
I like to hold you.
I'm glad you are a boy.
    or
I'm glad you are a girl.

Ask: *Are there any questions about what each of these mean?* (Refer to Chapter two in *Self-Esteem: A Family Affair,* and pages 256 and 257.)

✳

Say: **Visualization** *is a powerful tool for focusing our own energy.*

Ask: *Will you do a visualization to focus on the Affirmations for Being? Choose a person you want to visualize. Straighten or center your body and breathe deeply. Close your eyes and see that person. Watch how that person acts and looks as he believes:*
"Yes, I do have the right to be here. I belong here.
Pause
It is OK for me to need what I need. I have the right to be and to grow.
Pause
I like being the sex I am.
Pause
I'm growing my way at my speed.
Pause

I like myself. I don't have to prove myself or to push other people around to be noticed. I am lovable because I am me.

Say: *Come back now. People who like visual experiences find this easier than people who prefer auditory (hearing) or kinesthetic (feeling) experiences; so if your picture wasn't clear this time, don't worry.*

Ask: *Does anyone want to share anything about visualizing with the group, whether from your experience or from the reading on visualization, page 37 in the text?*

Say: *We will examine how these affirmations can be offered to an infant, a thirteen year old, and to an adult.*

Hand out a set of **Being** affirmation cymbals to each person or ask them to turn to page 49 in their text and to check each message that they hear included in the following three examples:

Say: *Imagine that you hear the cry of a tiny baby, eight-week-old Tommy. His parent goes to his crib, gently picks him up, and says in a soft, pleasant, leisurely voice: "Hello, sweet baby! Oh, you're wet. Well, here is a dry diaper. Have I told you today how delighted I am that you are a boy, Tommy? I'll tell you again, you wonderful fellow. You certainly are stronger and*

70

*bigger than you were last
week. Go ahead and grow at
your own speed; I like you
whatever size you are. You
are so cuddly—I love to rock
you!"*

Ask: *Was each of the affirmations
included? Do you think
babies understand what is
being said to them?*

Read Recycling definitions on page
272 in the text.

Say: *The recycling theory states
that teenagers recycle earlier
stages of development and
that many thirteen year olds
recycle the Being decisions.*

Say: *Will you visualize thirteen-
year-old Bill? He is usually a
rather grown-up,
independent kid. However,
like most thirteen year olds,
he often recycles birth to six
months tasks. He pushes to
check supply lines for food,
shelter, clothing, protection,
transportation, love, and
attention in ways that
appear to be juvenile
compared to his typical
behavior of the year before.
Tonight Bill asks for some
touching. Listen to Mom and
Bill and star the affirmations
or pick out the cymbals that
Mom offers to Bill.
Bill: "Mom, will you scratch
my back?"
Mom: "Sure, Bill, come here."
Bill: "No, I mean after I get
ready for bed."
Mom: "OK, come out here
when you are ready."
Bill: "No, I mean after I get*

*into bed."
Mom: "Oh, I see. OK, I'll
come in."
In the bedroom:
Mom: (scratching Bill's
back), "I don't get a chance
to do a backscratch and a
tuck-in very often, now that
you kids are all so big. I sure
do love you, Bill. I'm lucky to
have you for my son."*

Ask: *Which of the affirmations did
Mom give to Bill? Do you
think that Mom invited Bill to
decide that it is OK for him to
be?*

Say: *The following night, when
Bill's Mom asked if he
wanted a backscratch, he
acted insulted. But a few
days later he was hounding
his dad to wrestle and then
to tell a story about when he
was thirteen. As they recycle,
thirteen year olds often
alternate grown-up behavior
with very young behavior.*

Say: *Adults also recycle being.*

Ask: *Will you be yourselves, here,
today, and listen to the
affirmations and see if any
of them feels especially
comforting? I will read the
Affirmations for Being for
adults.*

Read the Affirmations for Adults,
page 50 in text, beginning "Hello, I
believe that you . . . ."

Ask: *Will you look at your
Affirmation cymbals, choose
the one or two that you want
to hear, ask someone near
you to read them to you, and*

then will you listen and let
them in?

Return to the Affirmation for Being
worksheet, pages 48 and 49 in text.
Assign these three items to do at
home.

Ask: *Will you choose another
person (child, spouse, or
friend) and at the left of each
affirmation write the way in
which you can convey it to
that person? You can use
words, touch, or a smile. The
Rewards for Being sheet, on
page 17 in the text, has
examples.*
*Young teens who are
recycling earlier stages may
be helped to resolve old
problems by these
unconditional love messages.
These Being messages are
especially important to hear
if one is ill or injured.
Messages must be sincere. If
you don't mean them, don't
say them. If you don't say
them, think about how to
become free to offer this kind
of Being nurturing to others
and mean it.*

Ask: *Will you write on the right
hand side of each
affirmation the way you
want to hear it and the
name of someone who might
give it to you? Find at least
three different sources for
your five affirmations. That
way you will keep several
options open and avoid
having all your eggs in one
basket.*

6. PARENTING TIPS
(0-20 Minutes)

Hold up the **Parenting Tips,** pages
44 and 45 in the text.

Ask: *Will you turn to Parenting
Tips, pages 44 and 45 in the
text?*

Ask: *Does anyone have a question
or comment to share about
the Parenting Tips or about
the readings in Chapters one
and two?*

Say: *Section IIB in Parenting Tips
for Raising a Birth to Six-
Month-Old Infant says, "The
adults nurture and protect
Jason. They care for the
baby in a gentle, loving way
that encourages him to be
joyful."*

Say: *The responsibility of the
adult caring for an infant is
to respond to the child, think
what he needs, and meet
those needs. The
responsibility of the infant is
to make his needs known.*

Ask: *Does anyone want a
Suggestion Circle on ways to
take care of yourself while
you are providing full-time
care for an infant?*

Say: *Section IIB tells how letting a
baby come to a full cry and
then responding to his needs
lays the groundwork for
independence and
responsibility.*

Ask: *Does anyone want a
Suggestion Circle on ways to
deal with other adults who*

pick your baby up the moment he makes a sound or who insist that it is good for babies to cry a long time?

Say: *Those of us who don't easily ask for what we want or need can improve our ability to ask as we recycle.*

Ask: *What are examples of things that some adults have difficulty asking for?*

EXAMPLE:
privacy, time, attention.

Say: *Think about each of the Being affirmations and consider whether it would help you to ask for what you need.*

Ask: *Will you turn to What You Stroke Is What You Get, pages 52 and 53 in the text?*

Say: *On page 53 write the name of an infant you know. In the top box write, "I will help nurture you." In the middle box write, "I will think for you." Fill in the bottom box with joyful Being messages for the baby.*

7. WHAT ARE STROKES? (20-25 Minutes)

Ask: *Will someone who has read about or knows about strokes explain what a stroke is?* Include: It is any kind of recognition—a word, look, touch, gift. It is anything that lets you know that the sender knows you are alive. If some people do not like the word "stroke," ask them to decide on a word that they would prefer such as "recognition" or "interaction" or "message" and to substitute that word for the word "stroke."

Ask: *Why are strokes important?*

Say: *Remember that strokes, like air, water, and food are necessary for health. Infants who are deprived of physical touching sometimes die of "marasmus."[5] As with food, different people have different stroke preferences.*

Say: *Affirmations are positive strokes. Some strokes are negative. The interaction exercise or Different Strokes for Different Folks will allow people to feel different kinds of strokes, to think about positive, negative, sincere and insincere strokes, and to think about the rules people have about giving and receiving strokes.*

Say: *I will read eight different ways of interacting with other people, for example, "Shake hands." I will ask you to role play each way without discussing it. Do think about how you would feel if you were doing this in a regular life situation.*

Say: *Because this is a role play, I may ask you to do some things that you do not usually (or ever) do, and you may feel phony or plastic at times. Please ignore any phony feelings and concentrate on thinking how you would usually feel if you were exchanging these kinds of recognition. Remember that you have the right to pass at any time.*

Ask: *Will you stand and do only what I tell you to do?*

Say the following sentences, leaving time between each for people to feel and think about the different kinds of strokes:

1. *Mill around and completely ignore each other.*
2. *Say some greeting, looking away.*
3. *Say some greeting with eye contact. Do not touch.*
4. *Touch arm, look in the eyes, smile, and say, "I'm glad you are in this class!"*
5. *Hug.*
6. *Give a cold, icy stare.*
7. *Say something irritable like, "I can't hear you—speak up!"*
8. *Put the palms of your hands against the palms of your partner's hands. Push each other firmly but not violently while repeating your irritable message.*

Reassemble the group in a circle.

Say: *Come back to your "here-and-now selves" and see the other people in the present. Give up any negative connection that you may have made with anyone in*

the room during the role play. If you want to say to someone, "I didn't mean what I said," do so now.

Pass out copies of the **Interaction** sheet, page 83.

Ask: *Will you take two minutes to number the Interaction items from number one, "I liked best," to number eight, "I liked least."*

Ask: *Will you share your two most liked interactions and your two least liked with the whole group?*

Record responses on newsprint with a felt pen.

Ask: *How many of you put a one or a two by "completely ignore?" A seven or an eight?*

Repeat for each item.

Say: *Variety in what people liked most and least is an example of the saying, "Different strokes for different folks."*

Ask: *Did anyone discover a stroke rule, a rule you have about giving or receiving strokes?*

OPTIONAL:
Give examples:
I can only give a compliment when it is sincere.
I don't believe that compliments from strangers are sincere.
I won't push another adult, but I sometimes hit children.
Men are not supposed to hug other men.

74

Women are not supposed to hug men (except husband, father, brother).

Record any rules mentioned and hold for the Strokes Rules list to be used in Meeting 4.

Say: *In review, strokes are any kind of interaction (positive or negative, sincere or insincere) between two people. And since strokes are essential for life, if people can't get enough positive strokes, they will get negative ones rather than go without.*

Ask: *How many of you know someone who seems to ask for negative strokes? We will talk more about that at further meetings.*

Ask: *Will you take this sheet home and fill in the rest of the columns and think about the rules you have about getting and giving strokes?*

Get report on eye contact homework.

Say: *Some people like eye contact. Will those of you who indicated at the first meeting*

✳ *that you were going to observe how often you used eye contact with members of your family tell us what you found?*

Say: *If most people in this group have the same rules about eye contact, that may indicate that we have similar cultural*

backgrounds. In some cultures people learn that it is "respectful" to look another person directly in the eye. In other cultures it is disrespectful.

OPTIONAL:
If stroke rules like "Don't touch because touching is sexual" surface, offer the group the Separating Sex and Nurturing exercises, Meeting 5, pages 149-151.

---

8. FIVE KINDS OF STROKES *(10-25 Minutes)*

Ask: *Will you look at the three balloon sheet that you did as*
✳ *homework? Will someone tell what messages you gave? Does anyone want to share an "I learned . . ."?*

OPTIONAL:
As he reports each message, hand him a red marble if it was for Being, a green marble if it was for Doing well, and a blue one if it was for Doing poorly (or Can-do-better). Repeat for two or three more people, depending on time.

Ask: *Will you look at and feel the marbles in your hand? Do you like the number of strokes you gave? The balance of colors?*

Say: *There are five kinds of strokes. You have already practiced the three that invite high self-esteem, that are affirming. There are two kinds of strokes that can tear down self-esteem. They are negations, or negative strokes, "Don't be" messages about Being, and Plastics, strokes that have some positive mixed with some negative.*

Ask: *Will you give an example of each?*

Review the five kinds of strokes. List them on the chalk board in chart form as people give examples.

STROKE	POSITIVE OR NEGATIVE	EARNED OR UNEARNED	EXAMPLE	PAGE IN TEXT
Being	positive	unearned	I like you.	17
Doing well	positive	earned	I like what you did.	18
Doing poorly	negative	earned	I don't like what you did.	19
Don't be	negative	unearned	Drop dead.	21
Plastic	negative	earned or unearned	You think well for a girl.	20

Say: *Will you turn to page 23 in your text? I will give you examples of the five kinds of strokes, and you put a mark on the balloon in which you think each belongs. Remember, do not believe the Don't be's and Plastics.*

1. *You follow directions very well.*
2. *Don't forget the Ground Rules. They offer us all protection. Use the right to pass whenever you want to.*
3. *If you were not here, I could be at the movies.*
4. *You are doing quite well for people with as many problems as you have.*
5. *I'm glad I'm getting to know you.*

Check the answers: 1. Doing
2. Doing poorly 3. Don't be
4. Plastic 5. Being

Ask: *Will you write on the outside of each balloon, on page 23 of the text, "earned" or "unearned"?*

Hold up your book and show page 23 already filled in with the examples you just read.

Ask: *Will you do the Five Balloon worksheet, page 23 in the text, for a period of fifteen or twenty minutes of a specific day? Write the name of the person for whom you will record strokes, the day of the week, and the time of the*

day. Count the strokes you give by recording them on the appropriate balloons.

Say: *If you hear yourself giving a Don't be or a Plastic, stop, take it back, and give a different one (Being, Doing well, Can-do-better) instead. Strokes are like kites: when I send one out, it has my string on it, and if I realize that I sent a message that I wish I had not sent, I can pull it back. I can do it immediately—"I didn't mean that, I meant this instead." Or I can write a letter, make a phone call, talk with the person at a later time.*

Say: *We will use this worksheet another way at our next meeting.*

9. ADDITIONS
Address any items added during goal setting.

CLOSING (10 Minutes)
Take care of any business details.
Hand out **class roster.**
Point to the **Goals** and briefly note the content covered.
Review things to do at home before the next meeting.

1. *OPTIONAL: Make a list of Things to Do Instead of Hitting.*
2. *Practice the Being Affirmations on someone else and on yourself. (Self-*

Esteem: A Family Affair, *pages 48, 49, and 50.)*

3. *Complete the Interactions worksheets.*

4. *OPTIONAL: Do the bottom box of What You Stroke Is What You Get, page 53, with loving words for an infant you know.*

5. *Fill in the Five Balloon sheet on pages 20-23 in text.*

6. *Read page 261 and Chapter six through page 173 in the text in preparation for learning about responsibility and how the individual's own values and structure are incorporated into the personality.*

Place a large card with the following **affirmations** on the floor.

AFFIRMATIONS
I have every right to be alive and competent.
It is OK for me to have needs, and I can see to it that my needs are met.
I'm glad that I am a man (woman).
I don't have to hurry and grow up or pretend to be young to be loved and cared for.

Ask: *Will you stand in a circle and read these Being Affirmations aloud?*

Ask: *Does anyone have Resentments? Appreciations?*

Say: *The meeting is closed. I'll see you next week/meeting. Thank you.*

Identifying Four Ways of Parenting

Write descriptive words on 3x5 white cards		Write examples of message on 3x5 colored cards

AFFIRMS

		"I love you."
Gives permission to do things well		"You are important to me."
Gives gentle, supportive care	NURTURING	Comforting hug
Invites person to get needs met		Encouraging smile
Gives affection		

Write descriptive words on 3x5 white cards		Write examples of message on 3x5 colored cards

AFFIRMS

Tells how to do things well		"Don't pull the kitty's tail, because you'll hurt the kitty. Pat her gently."
Assertive	STRUCTURING AND PROTECTING	"You are smart, You can solve it. Do it."
Sets limits		Stops young child from running into the street
Demands appropriate performance		Confronts chemical abuse
Offers tools		
Is capable		
Acts responsibly		

Write descriptive
words on
3x5 white cards

Write examples
of message on
3x5 colored cards

NEGATES

MARSHMALLOWING

Gives permission
to fail.

Subtly destroys

Smothers

Patronizes

Sounds supportive,
invites dependence

"Mommy will do it for you."
(Age 8)

"Chipper, dear, you're having
a hard time, aren't you?"

"Can't you think of ways to
get your friends not to be
mad at you anymore?"

Hugs too long

Smiles at destructive behavior

Write descriptive
words on
3x5 white cards

Write examples
of message on
3x5 colored cards

NEGATES

CRITICIZING

Tells how to fail

Tears down

Ridicules

Blames

Discourages harshly

"It's all your fault. You
should be a better father."

"Why do you always do that?"

"Is that all you ever think
about—yourself?"

Laughs at humiliation
and pain

Your Eggs Are Getting Cold

EXAMPLES:

Unclear: Your eggs are getting cold.

Clear: *Your eggs are cooked, and if you want warm eggs come and eat them now.*

Unclear: I've lost my book.

Clear: *Do you know where my book is?*

Unclear: The paper is not here.

Clear: *Did you bring the paper in this morning?*

Rewrite the following to indicate who is responsible for what.

1. The dishes look as if they are not done.

2. We need someone to give us a demonstration.

3. Is the dog hungry?

4. That picture is terrible.

5. What about the shower?

6. There are no clean socks in my drawer.

7. The checkbook is overdrawn.

8. Stand in front of a closed door, with your arms full of packages, looking forlorn.

9. Is Erin there?

10. The garbage man is coming in the morning.

11. I didn't hear your clarinet today.

12. There is no milk.

13.

14.

Your Eggs Are Getting Cold

1. The dishes look as if they are not done.

Do the dishes!

Will you do the dishes?

Did you do the dishes?

Help me with the dishes.

2. We need someone to give us a demonstration.

Who will give us a demonstration?

Brad, will you lead the demonstration?

3. Is the dog hungry?

Jim, feed the dog.

Did you feed the dog?

Mary, feed the dog before 5:00

4. That picture is terrible.

I will not put that picture in the family album.

Take the picture down off the wall and put it in the closet.

Will you fix the T.V. picture?

I don't look pretty in that picture. Will you take another?

I didn't like that motion picture plot.

5. What about the shower?

Will you take a shower?

Clean the shower when you are through.

Did you turn the shower off completely?

I want to take a shower. When will you be out?

Turn the shower off.

Who is planning the shower for Mary?

I will help plan the baby shower for Sandy.

6. There are no clean socks in my drawer.

I will wash my socks today.

Will you wash my socks.

Will you get me some clean socks?

When will you be doing my socks in the laundry?

Will you give me some money to buy some new stockings?

7. The checkbook is overdrawn.

I have overdrawn my bank account. I will deposit some money.

Will you deposit some money in our checking account?

Will you lend me some money?

Interaction

	Rank Order: (1) I liked best to (8) I liked least.	I felt: Glad, sad, mad, confused, lonely, happy, irritated, scared . . .	Rank Order: (1) I give most often (8) I give least often.
1. Mill around and completely ignore each other.			
2. Say some greeting, looking away.			
3. Say some greeting with eye contact. Do not touch.			
4. Touch arm, look in eye, smile and say, "I'm glad you are in this class!"			
5. Hug.			
6. Give a cold, icy stare.			
7. Say something irritable—"I can't hear you. Speak up!"			
8. Put the palms of your hands against the palms of your partner's hands. Push each other firmly but not violently while repeating your irritable message.			

Interaction

	Rank Order: (1) I liked best (8) I liked least	I felt: Glad, sad, mad, confused, lonely, happy, irritated, scared . . .	Rank Order: (1) I give most often (8) I give least often
1. Mill around and completely ignore each other.			
2. Say some greeting, looking away.			
3. Say some greeting with eye contact. Do not touch.			
4. Touch arm, look in eye, smile and say, "I'm glad you are in this class!"			
5. Hug.			
6. Give a cold, icy stare.			
7. Say something irritable—"I can't hear you. Speak up!'"			
8. Put the palms of your hands against the palms of your partner's hands. Push each other firmly but not violently while repeating your irritable message.			

Homework

1. Make a list of Things to Do Instead of Hitting. (optional)
2. Practice the Being Affirmations on someone else and on yourself. (*Self-Esteem: A Family Affair*, pages 48, 49, and 50.)
3. Complete the Interaction worksheets.
4. Do the bottom box of What You Stroke Is What You Get, page 53, with loving words for an infant you know. (optional)
5. Fill in the Five Balloon sheet on pages 20-23 in text.
6. Read in text, page 261 and Chapter six through page 173 in preparation for learning about responsibility and how the individual's own values and structure are incorporated into the personality.
7. Notice direct and indirect questions.

Notes

1. John Bowlby, *Child Care and the Growth of Love* (Middlesex, England: Penguin Books, Ltd., 1953).
2. Thanks to Nancy O'Hara for designing this exercise on identifying Four Ways of Parenting.
3. Thanks to Sally Dierks for designing the responsibility exercise, Your Eggs Are Getting Cold.
4. Pam Levin Landheer, *Becoming the Way We Are: A Transactional Guide to Personal Development* (Berkeley, Calif.: Transactional Publications, 1974).
5. Ashley Montagu, *Touching: The Human Significance of the Skin* (New York: Harper and Row, 1971).

LETTER TO MARJ 3

Dear Marj,

Happy Birthday Friday. I hope you have a delightful day. Do ask for celebration wishes from your class.

About lesson three—the class is a quarter over before the start of this meeting. If it seems as if you haven't covered a quarter of the material, that is correct. The first meetings take time for people to make connections with each other and with you. After that is done and the groundwork is laid, content can be covered faster. It is, after all, not the content but the people who are important. The content is there *for* the people, and it is important to the extent that it helps people solve their own problems.

You asked how to begin on time if everyone has not arrived. I watched LaDonna Hoy teach. She started exactly at 7:30, with some people not yet in the room. After handing out pieces of goldenrod-colored paper, LaDonna quietly asked each person to find a partner, make a name tag for her, and identify one or more ways in which she takes good care of other people. As soon as the first pair had finished, LaDonna asked them to tell what they had written about each other. Five minutes later, all sixteen people had been introduced.

LaDonna asked people to raise their hands to signify which Ground Rule they preferred, and two people explained why they had chosen the one they had. She finished by 7:40. That was a fast-moving first ten minutes. Everyone had spoken, everyone had received positive strokes, and two people had stated opinions. It wasn't hurried or rushed—she just kept moving gently along.

Wouldn't it be fun if someone in the group offered to take the goals posters home and make bigger, "funner," colored posters? If someone requests a Suggestion Circle or Four Ways of Parenting, do it at this time.

1. Post the definition of a stroke if you want to. Collecting these **Stroke Rules** was difficult for me when I didn't work quickly. Don't explain or expand on the theory at this point. Give out the paper; give one or two examples, and start to write your own list. Post the definition of a stroke, if you want to.

    Before the next meeting, combine the participants' lists with your own list and the rules you recorded during the Interaction exercise. Duplicate these and have them ready for use at the next meeting when the group will examine Stroke Rules.

2. **Five Kinds of Strokes** is a review in preparation for the Jelly Bean exercise. Listen carefully to be sure that people have

correctly identified the five kinds of strokes. When you ask people to answer questions in their minds you are using "internal interview."

I expect that you are familiar with this Values Clarification technique. If not, it is different from asking a rhetorical question to which there is supposed to be a right answer or to which you plan to give the answer. "Internal interview" is a silent interview—each person answers the questions internally only. I regulate the length of the pauses by doing the internal answering myself and then adding a bit more time to the pause. I like internal interviews because they are quick, private, and imply personal responsibility.

Ah, the **Jelly Beans**—my favorite exercise! I have done it many, many times and I still learn something about myself each time I do it. Encourage people to practice hearing and deciding about all five kinds of messages.

Group encouragement to throw away destructive messages can have a powerful effect for some people. Ann, an attractive woman, sweet to everyone and well-liked, was eating each **Don't be** and **Plastic** jelly bean. The group urged her not to keep them or at least not to eat them! I offered her a **Plastic.** She had started to put it in her mouth, when suddenly she picked up a dish of corn nuts and dumped it on top of my head. She looked startled, then apologetic, and then said, "No, I am not going to apologize!" Clap, clap, holler, holler, "Yeah Ann!!"

The Jelly Bean exercise is the heart of Meeting 3. It offers people a protected way to examine whether their stroke rules are working for them or against them.

3. **Three Parts of the Personality** is aimed at helping both children and adults become well-rounded personalities. If I need to shorten some of the content, I shorten this section.

If you are not sure whether you can identify behaviors that are typical of each part, look at the review of all Three Parts of the Personality in Meeting six, page 174. Read the cards for each part with feeling and observe your own behavior.

People who are familiar with Transactional Analysis will recognize that these exercises are applications of Ego State theory. If you want additional background reading, I recommend *Born to Win*[1] by Muriel James and *Egograms*[2] by John Dusay.

For the demonstration of the personality parts, make the circles ten inches in diameter or larger. On them write the words "Nurturing and Structuring," "Problem Solving," and "Spontaneous and Adaptive." Avoid using initials. Seeing whole words helps people learn.

The demonstration of the three parts sounds complex, but I watched Sheila Hartmann complete it in ten minutes. People reported the differences in posture, voice, and facial expression that they had observed. This is an introduction intended to give people a glimpse of the three parts, not a definitive picture. If you don't have a hand puppet—give balloons to both people who are playing.

4. Here you introduce the very important **Nurturing and Structuring Part.** When some people get involved in that part, they get critical, or at least very earnest. So will you breeze through this with some lightness?

Anything you can do to encourage people to improve the quality of their Nurturing and Structuring Part will benefit themselves and the people they care for. Emphasize that this is the part of the personality that holds morals, values, and traditions and that without it we would be amoral. Unfortunately, this part has been maligned because some people operate mostly in marshmallowing or criticizing ways, and I have heard the cry, "Get rid of shoulds!" Not so! Hold on to shoulds; improve their quality; check out their appropriateness. We need them to protect the Spontaneous Part of us and to make value judgments for the Problem Solving Part of us.

The **Good Mothers and Good Fathers** lists usually bring a lot of response from the group. Encourage people to remember that any rule on their list got there because at some time it was functional. I have done this exercise fifty times, I suppose, and each time I *enjoy* crossing off and rewriting rules. It reminds me that I can start using new rules at any time. Betty Beach took copies home for her children to revise so she could see how their ideas of a Good Mother compare to hers.

5. Do the **Four Ways of Parenting** at least once at every meeting. Do it quickly. Some people may be comfortable with this exercise by this meeting, but "comfortable" is not important. It may even equal "stagnant." Don't worry if they *or* you are uncomfortable with the role. Just go ahead and invite people to think and to grow. This is the last meeting plan in which I will include directions for doing the Four Parent. You can refer back to this set of directions for the remaining five meetings.

Here are some thoughts on leading the Four Parent exercise. I sabotage the exercise if I: change the question . . . let the question be too big or too fuzzy . . . let the listening person give so much content that people focus on the story instead of the problem . . . forget to ask the whole group to offer options . . . let it drag . . . let the speaking people get in front of the chair where the listening person can see them . . . forget to encourage nonverbals like a hand on the shoulder . . . forget to remind folks that there are many ways to give each of the responses and that the ones in the book are examples, not "right answers" . . . ask two questions, especially if they have opposite answers (example: "Do you understand or do you want the question repeated?")

Sometimes people have trouble understanding Nurturing. Maybe this thought will help: Nurturing is something that feels good, but it also has to be good *for* you. Using drugs feels good but it is not good for you, so sniffing coke is not, **not**, nurturing yourself.

6. This **Responsibility** exercise is designed to encourage responsibility for behavior in ourselves and in our children. Dick and I are considering starting a new business firm. First we will manufacture "Things That Fall into Place." You can buy a box containing large styrofoam things that you stick to the ceiling with special glue. You also get a signal set, maybe a garage door opener sort of gadget; and at the appropriate time, you push the buttons, and the things on the ceiling fall into place in a neat pattern on the floor. After we get that line selling well, we plan to add "Things That Turn Out Well"; and then we have thought about "Things That Just Don't Jell." If you get some ideas for good product lines, please let us know.

Anyway, move through this exercise quickly. It builds on Your Eggs Are Getting Cold. Usually it is greeted with groans and laughter as people recognize common phrases that are not intended to harm anyone but that invite irresponsibility and possibly a feeling of powerlessness.

7. Why study these **Affirmations** for six to twelve year olds now? you ask. Why not the next chronological set? Several reasons. These affirmations reinforce the teaching about the Nurturing and Structuring part of the personality. I believe that they are helpful to folks who are taking a class. In addition, when I introduce the six to eighteen month tips in Meeting 2 to a group of adults who deal mainly with older children, I sometimes hear, "I don't want to wait six weeks until I hear something for me." Of course that would not be true because we emphasize the Recycling theory, but people may not understand that yet. And since this is not a course on "child development," I see no reason to have a chronological sequence.

I make some decisions about how to present the Affirmations when I do the Goals. If there are folks who want Parenting Tips for six to twelve year olds, I do the section of Affirmations for the six to twelve year olds. If not, I skip ahead to the Affirmations for young adults and spend more time on the Affirmation worksheets in the text.

8. If you do the **Parenting Tips,** emphasize that this is the age at which adults should be challenging kids' rules and that it is an important investment of parent energy.

As we **close** this third meeting . . . notice whether people are telling their Resentments and Appreciations yet. A woman stayed after class to tell me all the things that she didn't like. When I said, "Will you say those things during Resentments time in our next meeting?" she said, "Oh, I didn't know we could do that." One class changed Resentments to Things I Don't Like because they felt that 'resentments' was too strong a word. I like it when people change things to get what they want and need. If I get Resentments about going too fast or offering too much material, the next week I ask for discussion about whether we want to change our contract—meet longer, more frequently for example. Generally, I prefer brisk meetings. I do not believe in staying on an exercise till we have extracted every meaning out of it. I trust people to get ideas and to take them home and think about them. Sometimes people take the class more than once, and that is fine.

Hope you run a superb meeting! Bye, and I wish you a whole bag of yellow jelly beans.
Love you,

Jean

MEETING 3

BEFORE MEETING 3

1. Study Meeting 3 plan.
2. Reread Chapter six in text and pages 261 and 264.
3. Reread "Who, Me, Lead a Group?" Question 2, Step 4.
4. Read the third Letter to Marj.
5. Collect the following **supplies:**
   paper for name tags
   felt tip pens
   tape
   whole sheets of paper
   half sheets of paper
   jelly beans
   balloons, hand puppet
   twelve-inch paper or plastic circles
6. Make or collect the following **visual aids:**

POSTERS
- Meeting 3 Goals, Meeting 3, page 93
- Ground Rules, Meeting 1, page 37
- Good Mothers and Good Fathers, Meeting 3, page 98
- All six Affirmation posters, Meeting 2, page 70; 3, page 101; 4, page 123; 5, page 151; 6, page 172; 7, page 199
- Closing Affirmations poster, Meeting 3, page 105

CARDS AND SIGNS
- Three Parts of Personality twelve inch circles:
  - Nurturing and Structuring
  - Problem Solving
  - Spontaneous and Adaptive
- Four Ways of Parenting signs, Marj 1, page 33

- Affirmations for Structure cymbals, Marj 2, page 58

DUPLICATED HANDOUTS
- Five Balloon sheet, Meeting 3, page 106
- Our Nurturing and Structuring Part, Meeting 3, page 108
- Things Are Falling into Place, Meeting 3, page 110
- Combined Good Mothers and Good Fathers list, Meeting 2, page 65
- How to Strengthen the Nurturing and Structuring Part, Meeting 3, page 109
- Homework, Meeting 3, page 111

OPENING (5-10 Minutes)

Post all the posters.

NAMES
Hand out name tags and felt pens.

Ask: *Will you work in pairs and make a name tag for your partner? Print her name and a way in which she takes good care of someone else. If you don't know her, ask her what she does to take good care of someone else.*

After three minutes . . .

Ask: *Will you introduce your partner and tell how she is good at taking care of other people? Who is willing to start?*

GROUND RULES
Point to the **Ground Rules** poster.

Ask: *As I read the Ground Rules poster, will you raise a hand to indicate which of the five ground rules you believe to be most helpful?*

Ask: *Will someone say how one of the rules is helpful for you?*

GOALS
Point to the **Meeting 3 Goals** poster.

MEETING 3 GOALS
1. Stroke Rules
2. Five Kinds of Strokes
   The Jelly Bean Exercise
3. Three Parts of the Personality
4. Our Nurturing and Structuring Part
   Good Mothers and Good Fathers
5. Four Ways of Parenting
6. Responsibility
7. Affirmations and Recycling
8. Parenting Tips
9. Additions
10. Celebrations

Read the goals and negotiate:
1. **Stroke Rules**—*We will collect data from this group about our own stroke rules.*
2. **Five Kinds of Strokes**—*We will look at our five balloon sheets and use jelly beans to practice giving, receiving, and rejecting the five kinds of strokes.*
3. **Three Parts of Personality**—*We will see what they are.*
4. **Our Nurturing and Structuring Part**—*We will update the messages to that part with the Good Mothers and Good Fathers lists and the Four Ways of Parenting exercise. Does anyone have a request for a Four Parent exercise?*
5. **Four Ways of Parenting**—*We will practice them.*
6. **Responsibility**—*We will emphasize that people, not things, are responsible for behavior. You may view "Things Are Falling into Place" as a responsibility exercise or as a communication sharpener.*
7. **Affirmations**—*We will give affirmations for nurturing and structuring, for getting ready to do things our own way whether we are six to twelve years old or older.*
8. **Parenting Tips**—*Does anyone want time to explore Parenting Tips on six to twelve year olds?*
9. **Additions**—*Does anyone have suggestions for topics to be addressed by a Suggestion Circle or a Four Parent?*
10. **Celebrations**—*Does anyone want to share a celebration or an awareness from last week? (Do this now.)*

1. STROKE RULES
(15 Minutes)

Ask: *Will someone review what a stroke is? (A unit of recognition.)*

Ask: *Does anyone want to share
further thoughts about the
Interaction exercise?*
(Limit to five minutes.)

Ask: *Did anyone list A to Z Things
to Do Instead of Hitting? Will
you share your list?*

✳

Say: *We all have rules about
strokes, or we wouldn't know
when to hit or not hit or
whom to hug or when to
withdraw.*

Hand out half sheets of paper.

Ask: *Will you write a list of rules
about strokes that you have
heard? It does not matter if
the rules are old or new,
false or true. Write about
giving them, getting them
and rejecting them.*
EXAMPLES:
Compliments from adults are
worth more than
compliments from children.
Husband's compliments
count more than all of the
others combined.
Compliments from another
businessman mean more
than ones from the minister.
You have to earn everything.
If you get a cricitism, you
have to keep it. It must be
true.

Write your own list.
After three or four minutes . . .

Say: *If you will hand in your lists
without your names on them,
I will combine the lists for us
to discuss at our next
meeting.*

2. FIVE KINDS OF STROKES
(15 Minutes)

Say: *We will do some sharing
from our Five Balloon sheets
and then practice the five
kinds of stroking by giving
and receiving or throwing
away jelly beans as tokens
of the five kinds.*

Ask: *Will you turn to page 23 in
the text and will two or three
people give Being examples
from your worksheet?
Include nonverbal examples.*

Continue for Doing well, Doing
poorly, Don't be and Plastics.

Ask: *If anyone gave a Don't be or
Plastic during the last week,
will you tell us how you took
it back?*

Ask: *Will you answer these
questions in your mind?*
● *Did I give most often the
kind of strokes I like best?*
● *Did I give most often the
kind I wish I got more of?*
● *Did I give the most of the
kind I like the least?*
● *Do I ask directly for the
kind I like best?*
● *Do I set myself up to get the
kind I like least?*

Say: *You can think what you will
do with this information.*

Ask: *Does anyone have further
thoughts or questions about
the worksheet?*

Say: *If you can't decide where a
particular communication
belongs, don't worry. The*

purpose of the Jelly Bean exercise is to provide a general picture of the strokes we give and of some we may want to change.

Say: *The Jelly Bean exercise makes strokes visible, showing number and kind of strokes we give, keep, or reject.*[3]

Place two **Five Balloon** sheets and a dish of jelly beans on the floor. Invite someone to demonstrate the exercise with you. Sit opposite her on the floor.

Say: *This is a role play. The purpose of the exercise is to experience getting and giving all five kinds of strokes, so I will give some sincere and some insincere ones.*

Say: *1. I will say or do something—send a stroke.*
2. You put a jelly bean on your balloon sheet indicating the kind of stroke that you heard or felt.
3. Then I will put a jelly bean on my sheet indicating the kind of stroke that I intended to give.
4. You decide if you want to keep the jelly bean or throw it away.

Give your partner all Five Kinds of Strokes. If she receives one in a different balloon from the one you were aiming for, point this out and do not make any judgments. Encourage her to throw away the Plastics and the Don't be messages. Continue about one minute and include a nonverbal stroke.

EXAMPLES:
"Thank you for doing this exercise with me."
"Don't be late in paying your bills or you will be charged an extra fee. Pay on time."
Smile.
"Drop dead."
"You are doing much better than I expected you would."
Invite her to give you some strokes.

OPTIONAL:
Repeat a stroke with different tones of voice and with different facial and body expression.

EXAMPLE: "Who is your barber?" (Being—I care about you.) "Who is your barber?" (Doing—You found a good barber.) "Who is your barber?" (Doing poorly—Terrible haircut.) "Who is your barber?" (Plastic—Sounds interested, voice and face are bored and disinterested.)

Ask people to arrange themselves in small groups of four or five. Hand out copies of the **Five Balloon sheet** and small containers of jelly beans, dried beans, noodles or peanuts to each group.

Ask: *In your groups of three or four will you give and get all Five Kinds of Strokes?*

Say: *Observe where they are received and from where strokes were sent. Think about Stroke Rules.*

95

Move from group to group and listen and give strokes for five minutes.
Call people back to the large group.

Ask: *What did you learn during the exercise? Did anyone think of a Stroke Rule that you did not include on your first list?*

Record new rules and add them to the lists of Stroke Rules, old and new, false and true.

Ask: *During the week will you think about how converting strokes, moving them from one balloon to another, is related to self-esteem?*

Say: *This was a role play. Give up any bad feelings you may have had while practicing different kinds of strokes.*

Say: *Let yourself be clear about the five kinds of strokes and how you keep and reject them.*

Ask: *Did anyone have fun with the Jelly Bean exercise?*

Offer extra copies of the Five Balloon sheet to people to take home. They can offer the Jelly Bean exercise to their families, if the families want to do it.

3. THREE PARTS OF THE PERSONALITY
(15-20 Minutes)

Say: *For ease in practicing ways of encouraging well-balanced personalities in*

ourselves and children, we will divide personality functions into three parts. We will use these three parts as we consider parenting options, practice communication skills, strengthen responsibility, and consider what personality development is appropriate at what age. The first part is the Nurturing and Structuring part of us that we have already used in the Four Parent exercise. We use that part of us to decide what we "should" do. The second part of us, the part that collects data, we will call the Problem Solving Part. And the part of us that reacts spontaneously or in old adaptive ways we will call the Spontaneous and Adaptive Part.

Place the three circles (**Nurturing and Structuring, Problem Solving, Spontaneous and Adaptive**) on the floor in different parts of the room.

Say: *I will ask six people to demonstrate different behaviors.*

Ask: *Will two people demonstrate the Nurturing and Structuring Part by standing near the Nurturing and Structuring circle and making a list of skills and qualities that you think a good teacher possesses? Will two of you stand near the Problem Solving circle and demonstrate that part as one of you interviews the other to find out all the places he has lived and the jobs he has held? Will two of you stand near the Spontaneous and Adaptive circle and will one of you blow up this balloon while the other tries to make you laugh with this hand puppet?*

Ask: *Will the rest of you observe how the behavior of the three couples differs?*

Allow the activity to continue for two or three minutes. Collect the hand puppet and the balloon.

Ask: *Will the demonstrators sit down now? Thank you for doing this demonstration for us. Each of the three personality parts has a set of attitudes, responses, behaviors, voice tones, facial expressions and body postures that are typical of that part.*

Say: *The people listing "goods" and "shoulds" about teachers were probably in the Nurturing and Structuring Part of their personalities. Will someone describe their behaviors or postures or facial expressions?*

List on the board behaviors identified, adding some of your observations. (See example, page 107 at end of this Meeting.)

Say: *The interviewer was doing a "data collection" activity and was probably in the Problem Solving Part of her personality.*

Ask: *Will someone describe the interviewer's behavior or posture while she was conducting the interview?*

List on the board the behaviors identified, adding some of your observations.

Say: *The people "playing" were probably in the Spontaneous or Adaptive Part of their personalities. Will you describe their behaviors or facial expressions?*

Say: *Each of the three parts is important and has special roles to play in a fully functioning personality. We can develop each part in ourselves and encourage a healthy balance of the three in our children.*

4. OUR NURTURING AND STRUCTURING PART *(15 Minutes)*

Say: *Today we will learn more about the **Nurturing and Structuring Part** of the personality. The content of the Nurturing and Structuring Part can come from many different sources. Each of us chose our nurturing and structuring messages from among all the messages that have been offered to us. Many messages come from adults who cared for us when we were young.*

Ask: *Will each of you think of the people who cared for you*

and had a lot of influence on you before age six?
EXAMPLE:
mother, father, older brother or sister, foster parent, aunt, uncle, grandparent, housekeeper, babysitter, nursery school teacher, television.

Ask: *How many people came up with one name? Two names? Three? Four? Five? More?*

Say: *In this culture children are usually raised by one or two or three caring adults. In some cultures a group of caring adults raises children. Either way, the messages children choose to internalize very early are potent and long-lasting. This is helpful because it gives security to individuals, and it gives our culture continuity. Our early messages resemble a storehouse of cassette tapes or video tapes that give order and structure to our lives. However, sometimes early messages are no longer functional. One of the ways we can keep ourselves healthy and functioning well is to pull out our old tapes, examine them, and decide whether we want to keep them the way they are or update them. We can practice one way of doing that now.*

Hand out the **Good Mothers** list and/or the **Good Fathers** list.

Say: *Here are the Good Mothers and/or Good Fathers lists*

that we wrote during our last meeting.

Ask: *Will you work in groups of three and update these items?*

Assign ten items to each group. Post the **Good Mothers and Good Fathers** poster.

Say: *Here are the directions. Look at each of the ten items individually.*

GOOD MOTHERS AND GOOD FATHERS
1. Cross out items you do not believe are true.
2. Star those that you think are important to keep.
3. Rewrite those that you want to change.
4. Add any rules that you think are important.

Remember that these are individual rules. We will not all cross out or star the same ones or add the same new rules. There will not be a right or a wrong list.

After three minutes . . .

Ask: *In groups will you compare what you did with each item? Listen to each other. It is not necessary to agree. Remember the right to pass.*

After eight minutes . . .

Ask: *Will one person from each small group share one*

98

awareness with the large group?

Say: *Thank you for the list, and thank you for your participation. I invite you to take the list home and continue to create your updated list of Good Mothers and Good Fathers rules. The Good Mothers and Good Fathers list is an example of nurturing and structuring tapes. You can see how some other people did this exercise by looking at pages 24 and 26 in the text.*

Pass out copies of **Our Nurturing and Structuring Part** sheet and **How to Strengthen Your Ability to Nurture and Structure.**

Say: *Here are two sheets for you to take home and use if you want to. One gives further information on our Nurturing and Structuring Part and the other suggests ways to strengthen that part.*

5. FOUR WAYS OF PARENTING *(5 Minutes)*

Say: *The Four Ways of Parenting exercise demonstrates the positive and negative ways in which the Nurturing and Structuring Part can be used.*

If you did not do a Four Ways of Parenting exercise at the start of the meeting, use a topic someone offers or use one of the illustrations from the text, pages 169 and 170. Hold up the **Four Ways of Parenting** signs.

Ask: *Will someone volunteer to play the role of the listening person? Will four of you wear the **Nurturing, Marshmallowing, Criticizing,** and **Structuring** signs and play the four sending roles?*

Remind people of the right to pass.

Ask: *Will you, the listening person, sit on the chair, and listen while the four sending people stand behind you and read the responses? Will you listen to all four, then identify which you like the best, and ask for any changes you want? Remember, you can turn the volume up or down like a radio.*

Do the role play.
Play all four roles yourself if necessary.

Ask: *Does anyone have anything you want to add to one of the responses? There are many ways to give each of the responses. The ones in the book are suggestions. Will each of you appreciate your own willingness and ability to role play different ways of parenting? Will you take off your sign and separate yourself from the role you were playing, if it was a negative role? Does anyone want another Four Ways of Parenting exercise?*

If so, do it.
Collect the signs.

99

Say: *Thank you. Each of us can develop good control of the volume on our messages. Sometimes we need better program material, that is, healthier messages. We can get these by listening to our inner wishes to be warm nurturers and helpful structurers, by observing other parents, by reading, and by attending parenting groups.*[4]

6. RESPONSIBILITY
(15 Minutes)

Say: *We are continuing the exercises on Responsibility.*

Ask: *Will someone who has practiced asking direct questions, instead of saying "Your eggs are getting cold," give us an example of how you did that?*

Say: *This Responsibility exercise is called Things Are Falling into Place.*[5] *It focuses on communications that imply that things, not people, are responsible for behavior. This skill is important to use with three to six year olds in helping them separate reality from fantasy. It is also important for six to twelve year olds because it encourages responsibility. It is significant for thirteen to nineteen year olds because it contributes to the sanity of their parents.*

Say: *One way to encourage responsibility in children and in ourselves is to remember that **people** are responsible for behavior.*

Hand out a copy of the **Things Are Falling into Place** list to each person.

OPTIONAL:
If short of time, divide into groups of three and have each group rewrite three or four items on the list.

Ask: *Will you rewrite the items on the list to invite people to be responsible for their behavior?*

Look at the first three examples.

Say: *After you have rewritten your list, move into groups of three and tell each other how you rewrote the items.*

Reassemble people into a circle.

Ask: *Will someone who rewrote item four read your new item for the whole group?*

Repeat for all the items.

Ask: *Did any of you think of other phrases we use that unintentionally invite irresponsibility?*

If so, add them to the list.

Say: *Between now and our next meeting, notice whether you use words to invite irresponsibility. If you do, think of what you can say instead. We invite self-*

esteem in children when we encourage them to make responsible statements and ask clear questions.

7. AFFIRMATIONS AND RECYCLING
(15 Minutes)

Point to the six **Affirmation** posters.

Ask: *Does anyone have thoughts, feelings, or opinions they want to share about affirmations?*

Point to the **Being** poster.

Ask: *Did anyone find a way to use the Affirmations for Being on page 49 in the text?*

Say: *If you have trouble accepting Affirmations for Being, you may have a rule that you must earn all compliments. If so, you can decide to take a few compliments each day without earning them.*

Say: *The affirmations that we will study today support and strengthen our Nurturing and Structuring Part. They are the Affirmations for Structure or Learning to Do Things Our Own Way. They enhance self-esteem in six to twelve year olds and in all of the rest of us.*

Point to and read the **Affirmations for Structure** poster:

> **AFFIRMATIONS FOR STRUCTURE**
> You can think before you make that your way.
> Trust your feelings to guide you.
> You can do it your way.
> It's OK to disagree.
> You don't have to suffer to get what you need.

Say: *The Learning to Do Things Our Own Way or Affirmations for Structure are important for six- to twelve-year-old children, persons in late teens and early twenties, persons of any age who are entering new social settings such as organizations, businesses, recreation groups, or a new family. They are important for those retiring and for everyone else who is updating values and skills.*

Ask: *When a child thoroughly believes—incorporates—each of these affirmations, which one will help her . . .*
- *to be an independent thinker?*
- *to figure out what to do in a situation in which she has no past experience?*
- *to resist peer pressure?*
- *to be responsible for her morals and values?*
- *to resist when the kids say, "Everybody smokes, have one!"?*
- *to ask for help before a situation gets really bad?*

Ask: *Does "It's OK to disagree" mean that it is OK for a child to disagree with her parents? Does "You can do it your way" mean that her parents should let her do anything she wants to?*

Ask: *Do you have questions about the meaning of these affirmations?* (Encourage people to arrive at their own answers.)

OPTIONAL:
1. You can think before you make that your way . . . This is the protection against peer pressure.
2. Trust your feelings to guide you . . . through a situation in which you do not have enough facts to make a decision. Ask your feelings, your body, to give you a feeling—a clue about what to do.
3. You can do it your own way . . . Six to twelve year olds must start to find their own independent ways to do things in order to be ready to separate from their parents in the next stage.
4. It's OK to disagree . . . to think of alternatives, to find your independence. You may not always be able to act upon your disagreement, but you can know that you disagree.
5. You don't have to suffer to get what you need . . . You can ask for help before you get a headache or become

overtired. (More on page 261 in text.)

Hand out packets of **Affirmations for Structure** cymbals or slips of paper so people can copy them.

Ask: *Will you move into groups of three or four, pick out the message that you would like to hear, and ask someone to read it to you?*

Say: *Will each person choose a child between six and twelve? Think about that child—**visualize** the child in your mind; and after each affirmation is read aloud, say it silently to that child and think of how that child might respond.*

Read the Affirmations.

Say: *The Affirmations for Structure are appropriate for a young person who is in his late teens or early twenties.*

Ask: *Will you visualize a young person in her late teens or early twenties who is about to move away from her family and start a new job? Listen to the messages: "Congratulations on your new job. You will find that your company has many rules, some written and some unwritten. You can decide if they are right for you. If you feel uncomfortable with some of the rules, don't ignore that discomfort. Figure out a way to maintain your own values and independence. You can* disagree and learn to make your disagreements known in ways that help you and other people to grow. Find healthy ways to meet your needs. You don't have to be miserable."

Ask: *Which of these messages helped you?*

Say: *These Affirmations for Structure are for an adult who is going into a new family situation (marriage, divorce, additional child, child leaving).*

Ask: *Will you imagine a specific change in your own family structure? Listen to the messages: "Your family situation is going to be different now. That will cause some changes in your life. You may need some new methods for getting along in a different family pattern. You already have lots of methods in your head. So do the other members with whom you are living. You don't have to use those rules just because you already know them. You can think which ones will work best for you. When you disagree with other people, you can search for common ground. It is important to work out rules that you all feel agreement with. Talk openly about your needs and arrange to get them met. Don't wait until you have a headache or feel depressed. You are resourceful and you*

can build a satisfying family life."

Ask: *Which messages helped you?*

Turn to the Affirmations for Structure worksheets, pages 171, 172, and 173 in the text.

Ask: *Will you fill in page 172 for someone you know and for yourselves? Will you practice getting and giving those messages before the next meeting?*

Say: *Remember, give them only if you mean them!*

OPTIONAL:

8. PARENTING TIPS:
(5 Minutes)

Turn to the Parenting tips for raising the six- to twelve-year-old child, pages 167-168 in the text.

Ask: *Are there any thoughts or questions about these Parenting Tips or Chapter six?*
These affirmations are for a six to twelve year old. She is busy experimenting with different ways of doing and thinking, and she is claiming some of those ways as her own. She is comparing how things are done at her house with methods used at other houses. She is deciding which rules to incorporate as her own. Another way of saying this is that it is the job of the six to twelve year old to strengthen the

Nurturing and Structuring Part of her personality. That part will help her to define what she wants and needs and to acquire the skills necessary to meet her needs.

Say: *"You can do it your way" does not mean to give the child permission to do something dangerous or anti-social. Many adults have this fear, and children often have it also. That is why it is important for parents of six to twelve year olds to:*
1. *Monitor the kinds of things that children are allowed to do in their own way*
2. *Set necessary limits for protection and be firm about them*
3. *Do Healthy Hassling with the kids about the decisions they are making, pages 155-159, 167, and 170 in the text.*

Do a Suggestion Circle on ways to hassle the global statements kids make. Remember, the aim of Healthy Hassling is not to win or lose or even to be sensible but to challenge thinking. This kind of hassling is fun, not critical.

Ask: *Will someone suggest an idea for the Suggestion Circle, "How can I hassle in a uncritical way a kid who says_____"? Use your own example or use one of the following:*
1. *"I am ten, and I don't ever have to pick up any dishes again, because it is not important to me."*

2. *"I hate plaid shirts. I am not going to wear a plaid shirt . . . ever!"*
3. *All new houses should be built with fireplaces.*

EXAMPLE of Suggestion Circle question: "What can I say to hassle a kid who says, 'When I have my own apartment, I am never going to make the beds.' " Some responses could be: "Will you change the sheets, ever?" "If you have a party and want people to put their coats on your bed, will they put the coats on your sheets?" "If an overnight guest makes your bed will you invite her back?" "Will you allow your children to play at the house of friends who make their beds?"

Say: *Section IIIB on page 167 of the text says that parents of six to twelve year olds can use hassle time with their children to* **rethink long-unexamined rules** *and ways of doing things.*

Ask: *Do any of you have an old rule or way of doing things that you are glad you reexamined? Do you want to share the rule or how you changed it?*

Say: *One of the ways of encouraging responsibility in children of six to twelve is careful attention to clear* **rules with consequences.** *Logical consequences can be related to the material aspect of the problem.*

104

EXAMPLE:
"Forgot to put the bike away?"
"Can't ride for two weeks."

Say: *Logical consequence can also relate to the feelings or inconvenience of other people.*[6]

EXAMPLE:
Danny forgot to call home when he stopped at Cecil Bishop's house to play after school. When he came home an hour later, his mother explained that she had been worried, and that further, she expected him to think of something to do for her that would "make up for her" the time and energy she had spent worrying.

Ask: *Will any of you who use either kind of logical consequence share some of your experiences with the group?*

9. ADDITIONS

Address any items added during goal setting.

CLOSING *(10 Minutes)*

Point to the **Goals** poster and briefly note the content covered. Take care of any business details. Review the homework for the next meeting:

1. *Practice the Jelly Bean exercise if you want to.*
2. *Expand your Good Mother and Good Father list if*

you want to, and study the two Nurturing and Structuring sheets.
3. *Continue to practice the birth to six months Affirmations for Being (pages 48, 49, and 50 in text). Practice the Affirmations for Structure on somebody (pages 171, 172, and 173 in text).*
4. *Encourage responsibility by speaking in ways that indicate that people are responsible for behavior, not things.*
5. *Read Chapter four and pages 258 and 259.*

Place a large **Affirmation** poster on the floor.

AFFIRMATION
I know lots about families and I can think and feel which parts of this class I will use in my family.

Ask: *Will you stand and read the closing Affirmation with me?*

Read it.

Ask: *Will you find a partner and say this affirmation to each other? "You know lots about parenting and you can think and feel which things from this class you want to use."*

Ask: *Does anyone have Resentments? . . . Appreciations?*

Say: *The meeting is closed. I'll see you next meeting.*

Five Balloon

Behaviors Typical of the Three Parts of the Personality

NURTURING AND STRUCTURING PART	PROBLEM SOLVING PART	SPONTANEOUS AND ADAPTIVE PART
Writing a "should" list:	Taking a survey:	Playing with balloons and puppet:
weight on one foot	voice calm	giggling
hand on hip	posture straight	shouting "wow!"
head tilted	attitude business-like	demanding "Look!"
looking at each other sideways	head level	jumping up and down
soliciting "Don't you think..."	looking at each person's face	waving arms in air
arguing	"Will you tell me..."	smiling
frowning—sometimes pointing finger	face rather serious	gleeful
loud voice	using paper and pen	sad when balloon pops
		sitting on floor
		crawling over chairs
		grabbing each other's balloons

Our Nurturing and Structuring Part

1. The Nurturing and Structuring part of us contains a lot of rules about "how to" and "when to" and "what to do."
2. It is important because we use it to take care of other people and ourselves.
3. It provides structure and sets limits.
4. It is automatic and contains our "shoulds" and "oughts."
5. It is the repository of ethics and morals.
6. It is learned, often early, from other people or from our own past experiences.
7. It is important because the automatic parts, such as tying shoes without thinking about it, free us to do other things.
8. It is positive if the "how to's" are appropriate, and it is negative if they are no longer appropriate. It is positive if our nurturing helps us and other people to grow and negative if it creates dependence. It is positive if the judgmental part protects other people and ourselves and negative if it diminishes self-esteem.
9. It is important to remember that uncomfortable feelings may accompany changing old "shoulds." When one practices new attitudes or behavior it is not uncommon to feel awkward, uncomfortable, or even phony at first. It is important to accept those feelings as friends because uncomfortable feelings discourage us from changing too quickly and discarding helpful behavior and attitudes.
10. Six- to twelve-year-old human beings are especially busy developing independent internal structure strong enough to take care of themselves in a variety of situations. They do this by testing rules and arguing about beliefs and behavior.

How to Strengthen Your Ability to Nurture and Structure

1. Update old rules and skills.
2. Learn new rules and skills.
3. Take care of someone or something.
4. Take responsibility for something.
5. Do the Responsibility exercises.
6. Take care of yourself.
7. Do a Four Ways of Parenting exercise.
8. Separate sex and nurturing.
9. Affirm yourself for doing things your own way.
10. List twenty-five ways in which you are a good mom/dad/teacher/etc.
11. Write a letter to yourself about how to take care of yourself. Read it. Post it on your mirror. Do it!
12. Write a letter asking someone else to take care of you. Read it. Ask!
13. Write and say specific affirmations that you need.
14. Find positive role models.
15. Take a parenting class.

Things Are Falling into Place:

Unclear: The directions got up on the board.
Clear: *Sue put the directions on the board.*

Unclear: There are pieces that need to be picked up.
Clear: *Will you help me pick up these pieces?*

Unclear: There are fifteen minutes left.
Clear: *You have fifteen minutes to play before dinner.*

1. Things are making sense.

2. It had me discouraged.

3. This party could get out of control!

4. I hope the book helps

5. Has the newspaper come in yet?

6. Her life has fallen apart.

7. How much bantering should there be?

8. By that time, a new idea may have jelled.

9. Things are clicking now.

10. How did your day go?

11. Things are falling into place.

People, not things, are responsible for behavior.

Homework

1. Practice the Jelly Bean exercise if you want to.
2. Expand your Good Mother and Good Father list if you want to, and study the two Nurturing and Structuring sheets.
3. Continue to practice the birth to six months Affirmations for Being (*Self-Esteem: A Family Affair*, pages 48, 49, and 50). Practice the Affirmations for Structure on somebody (pages 171, 172, and 173 in text).
4. Encourage responsibility by speaking in ways that indicate that people are responsible for behavior, not things.
5. Read Chapter four and pages 258 and 259.

Notes

1. Muriel James and Dorothy Jongeward. *Born to Win: Transactional Analysis with Gestalt Experiments* (Reading. Mass.: Addison-Wesley. 1971).
2. John Dusay. *Egograms* (New York: Harper and Row. 1977).
3. Thanks to Bernadine Gradous for her help with the Jelly Bean exercise.
4. Thanks to Judy Howard for this description of the Four Ways of Parenting exercise.
5. Thanks to Title I parents of the Hopkins Public Schools and to Jan Schneider (Things Are Falling into Place).
6. Thanks to Laurie and Jonathan Weiss for introducing the author to logical consequences based on feelings.

LETTER TO MARJ 4

Dear Marj,

Mary Cleary says that the course "suddenly makes sense" during the fourth meeting. I have had a group tell me this during the third, fourth, or fifth meeting. There is a turning point in the process. People seem to become a team, to stop expecting the course to be perfect, to take responsibility for finding what they need, to support each other without doing the work for each other, and to cheer each other for going in individual directions. It is exciting; it is gratifying; and it marks a switch of energy expenditure. Until this point you may have been providing more energy than the group has. From now on they will provide more and more energy as you supply them with new tools, which they will take, try, judge, keep or discard and say, "What's next?" or "Have you a way to . . . ?"

It is your job to **start** on time. If people come late, that is their business. Absorb them, but do not slow the class in any way. This **name** exercise is a respect builder. List six or eight problem solving methods accurately, because you will use them when you explore the Problem Solving Part of the personality.

This time you focus on how **Ground Rules** offer protection for creativity. And remember that you can add Goals. This gives permission to other people to do so and lets them practice things they want to do. Example: "I am uncomfortable giving negatives for Doing, and I want to practice giving them in a constructive way." Ask how many people would be willing to practice with you, and fit a short practice session into Discounting or Stroke Rules. Do some time planning as you go through **Goals.** I often compress some things and expand others, but I believe it is important to always refer to last week's homework, so I don't skip that.

If people express an urgent request for Parenting Tips, I ask them to go through the first three Goal activities very quickly, and then I do Parenting Tips and the Suggestion Circle and Four Ways of Parenting to respond to specific questions.

Use the Suggestion Circle when a person seems to want alternatives or information. Use the Four Ways of Parenting when he seems to feel discouraged, helpless, or fearful. This exercise provides protection and offers optional new rules. Be sure to do at least one at every meeting. John Yetzer says that substituting Structuring for Marshmallowing is important because "You cannot humor a child into adulthood."

1. If people seem to grasp the idea of the Nurturing and Structuring Part of the personality, I keep that review very short. However, if people are saying, "I can't change—too uncomfortable," then the shoe tying exercise can help them. Keep your group in mind as you choose how much of this to do.

   The very important **Problem Solving Part** of us deserves careful treatment as this is the only part of our personality that does problem solving in the here and now. Any way that you can help people strengthen their problem solving ability will add to their coping skills. If I hear a discount like "I am no good at thinking," I say "I doubt it." I know all people have functional problem solving abilities, or they would not be in the group.

   This particular exercise may look long because it takes some space to describe it. Actually, each of the four parts of it is simple to do, and each can be done in about five minutes. (If people want time on Parenting Tips you might only use a couple of tips. Invite them to read the rest.)

   Karen West used Centering to change her posture, from slumped to straight. Then she changed her behavior from apologetic to competent and then her feelings from powerless to powerful. When Shirley Bullock noticed that someone who was trying to stand centered had his knees locked, she gave him a gentle push. She told him that when his knees are locked, he not only keeps his energy from flowing freely but that he is easy to push over. After he loosened his knees, she gave him another gentle push. His "Wow" registered surprise and appreciation.

2. **Affirmations for Thinking** fascinate me. They seem so indirect. Rather than "Think clearly" or "Be rational" there is "I'm not afraid of your anger." Sometimes I forget that the capacity to think develops freely only when we take care of feelings first.

   A father said, "I know that it is important to believe affirmations before I give them. How can I believe that I am not afraid of my son's anger when I am afraid of my own anger?" How indeed? Time to refer to therapy.

3. Eat Your Beans for Mommy is an exercise that leads straight to the heart of **who is responsible for whom.** This is a role play, and we write the messages on 3x5 cards. A woman who decided to feel guilty because she recently had said the exact words written on her card took comfort when she asked the other people in the class if they had ever said that stuff and they ALL, including me, said yes. She allowed the ensuing laughter to dissolve her guilt and went about the business of learning more responsible ways to talk to her little girl. Perhaps one reason this exercise is so effective is that it includes many different learning modes: listening, seeing, talking, writing, and moving about.

4. **Parenting Tips** for parents of the eighteen-month to three-year-old child is an optional exercise. Do anything you can to help change the label on two year olds from "negative" or "terrible twos" to "terrific twos."[1] "Negative" has so many connotations which encourage anger and distance between people.

   If some parents in your group are distressed by what they term "negativism" of two year olds, they may find the discussion questions helpful. These introduce the idea that two year olds need to separate from their nurturing adults and explore ways to express anger.

   I believe that either preventing two year olds from expressing their anger noisily or giving in to their angry outbursts invites them to say no inappropriately. This will mean a more difficult recycling job around age fourteen.

   Independent people have to know how to say "no." Ponder the plight of an eight year old, a fourteen year old, or a twenty year old who has never learned to say "no!"

5. Hurray! Today you get to do the **Stroke Bank Theory!** *My* bank, *my* feelings, *my* responsibility! This theory helped me lay to rest that irresponsible urge to insist, "You made me feel . . . ."

   People will be very specific about what their Stroke Bank levels are. Accept whatever they say. If you suspect that someone is lying, that is his business. Stay out of it. But keep the protection of the Ground Rules operating. Be free to ask for strokes and raise your own Stroke Bank level. It's good modeling, and also, it feels great!

6. When **Discounting** theory was presented all in one chunk, it was often discounted all in one chunk, and that was the end of that. Therefore, you will find the theory presented in small pieces, in the hope that it will help people accept what they need to change.

7. **Stroke Rules** are the heart of this lesson and the core of the rules by which we view ourselves and run our lives. The Family Mobile exercise is included here as a demonstration of the concept of family systems and of the idea that each person in the family influences the family system. Each family member can improve the quality of living experiences he is offering to others and to himself. Stroke Rules can enhance or limit that quality. Examine the list of rules carefully before you present this to the group. If you don't bash straight into a dysfunctional rule of your own, you will probably be the first person who hasn't. If you hear yourself stutter and say, "Yes, but . . . ." and "Don't you think . . . ?" ahead of time, you can be more accepting of other people's surprise. And you will be able to keep your own biases out of the group or at least to recognize them and claim them for what they are. Good Luck! And don't get

hooked into a "sincere" and "phony" argument, for this can be a way to avoid looking at rules. It is OK for people to pass. It is not OK for you to let people pull you around the bush and off the track.

Encourage people to write new rules. Let's say that I have an old Stroke Rule that says, "Only accept strokes for things done perfectly." That is keeping me from accepting lots of good strokes. However, if I junk that rule, I am throwing away something which has been part of me for a long time. So I will need a new strong Protecting and Nurturing message to replace it saying, "I am a worthwhile person, and I am lovable even when I am not perfect." I believe that is is unfair to invite people (including myself) to "get rid of" a message—even if it looks destructive—until they have identified a better message to put in its place. Remember: we do not take away all Stroke Rules! We write healthier ones.

Close on time. Resentments first, Appreciations last.

You are halfway through the course! This is a good time for you to think about the individual goals that people stated at the first meeting. Some people may have already moved beyond their original goals.

How about you? Are you making the course work for you? I hope so.

Love you,

Jean

MEETING 4

BEFORE MEETING 4

1. Study Meeting 4 plan.
2. Reread Chapter four in text and pages 258, 259, and 264.
3. Read the fourth Letter to Marj.
4. Reread "Who, Me, Lead a Group?", Question 6.
5. Collect the following **supplies:**
   paper for name tags
   felt tip pens
   pins or masking tape
   chalkboard or newsprint
6. Make or collect the following **visual aids:**

POSTERS
- Goals for Meeting 4, page 118
- All six Affirmation posters, Meeting 2, page 70
- Ground Rules, Meeting 1, page 37
- Stroke Bank, *Self-Esteem: A Family Affair*, page 109

CARDS AND SIGNS
- Eat Your Beans for Mommy, Meeting 4, page 124
- Three Parts of the Personality circles, Meeting 2, page 96
- Optional: A Family Mobile
- Affirmation cymbals for thinking, Marj 2, page 58
- Walter's responses, Meeting 4, page 129

DUPLICATED HANDOUTS
- Stroke Rules collected from Meeting 3, page 94
- Our Problem Solving Part, Meeting 4, page 131

- How to Strengthen the Problem Solving Part, Meeting 4, page 132
- Discussion Questions, Meeting 4, page 133
- Homework, Meeting 4, page 134

OPENING *(10 Minutes)*
Post the posters.

NAMES
Hand out name tags and felt pens.

Ask: *Will you work in pairs and choose a person different from last week's partner? Print a name tag for your partner, and write words that describe how that person solves a problem.*

Ask: *Will you introduce your partner and read one or two of that person's problem solving methods? List several of the problem solving methods on the board or on newsprint with a felt pen.*

GROUND RULES

Ask: *Will someone identify a Ground Rule that gives permission to think about problems in new ways?*

Refer to the **Ground Rules** poster.

GOALS

Point to the **Goals** poster

```
MEETING 4 GOALS
1. The Three Parts of the
   Personality
2. Affirmations for
   Thinking
3. Responsibility
4. Parenting Tips
5. Stroke Bank Theory
6. Discounting
7. Stroke Rules
8. Additions
9. Celebrations
```

Read the goals and negotiate.

1. ***The Problem Solving Part of the Personality***—*We will learn about the second part of the personality and how to strengthen our ability to think. Centering—We will practice centering as a way to support the Problem Solving Part of the Personality.*
2. ***Affirmations for Thinking***—*We will practice more of them.*
3. ***Responsibility***—*We will practice communication skills for taking responsibility for thinking and feeling. The exercise is called, Eat Your Beans for Mommy.*
4. ***Parenting Tips***—*Does anyone want time to discuss tips for eighteen-month to three-year-old children?*
5. ***Stroke Bank***—*We will learn the theory.*
6. ***Discounting***—*We will identify the three areas in which people discount.*

7. ***Stroke Rules***—*We will examine and update Stroke Rules, old and new, false and true.*
8. ***Additions***—*Are there any suggestions for topics to be addressed by a Suggestion Circle or a Four Parent?*
9. ***Celebrations***—*Does anyone want to share a celebration or an awareness? (Do so now.)*

1. THE THREE PARTS OF THE PERSONALITY (25 Minutes)

Place the Three Parts of the Personality signs on the floor.

Say: *At our last meeting we described the Nurturing and Structuring Part, which is the part of our personalities we use when we are nurturing, being ethical or moral.*

Ask: *Will someone stand on the Nurturing and Structuring Part sign and tell us a few things you remember about that part of the personality, such as why it is important and how to strengthen it?*

If no one offers, you do it.

Say: *The Nurturing and Structuring Part is important because: it gives structure to life, it is the repository of ethics and values, and it frees people to think about other things while they use automatic skills. Tapes stored in the Nurturing and Structuring Part are dysfunctional if they no*

118

longer work for the person's welfare. We can put new, functional messages on top of them, even if we are uncomfortable while we do this.

Ask: *Does anyone have anything to add? Do you have comments or questions about the handout sheet on the Nurturing and Structuring Part?*

Ask: *Will someone tell one thing you did to strengthen your manners, morals, or ability to nurture well?*

✱

OPTIONAL:

Say: We will do an exercise to experience the strength of old nurturing and structuring tapes.

Ask: Will you do the following activities and think about your feelings while you are doing them?

Untie your shoe and retie it. Untie your shoe again and tie it in the opposite way. (Make the other loop first, etc.)

Ask: How did you feel as you tied your shoe in an unfamiliar way?

Write the feeling words on the board or newsprint. Words frequently heard are: "awkward," "dumb," "excited," "angry," "interested," "challenged," "irritated."

Say: When people update old Nurturing and Structuring Part tapes (including Good

Mother or Good Father rules or Stroke Rules), they sometimes feel elated and excited. They may feel any of the feelings people had about tying shoes backward.

Say: *Today we will identify and strengthen the Problem Solving Part of the personality. There are four parts to this exercise.*

Part one:

Point to the list of **Things People Do When They Have a Problem to Solve** from the name tag exercise, Meeting 4, page 117

Ask: *Which items are examples of gathering and considering data?*

Circle the data-gathering items.

Ask: *Which items are examples of estimating probability, that is, deciding which solutions are the most likely to be effective?*

Underline those items.

Ask: *Which items indicate problem resolutions?*

Star those items.

EXAMPLES:

Talk with other people.

Go for a walk and think.

Think about what led up to the problem.

Listen.

Ask other people what they think.

Mull it over.

Find some authority.

Think what you did when you had a problem like this before.

* Do it.

Decide what would work.

Lie awake and worry.

Cry a lot.

(Ask the other people involved.)

Take the path of least
resistance. (This could be
probability estimation)

(Go to the library.)

Eat.

Say: *You already have a
functioning Problem Solving
Part. The identifying and
sorting that we just did are
examples of the way you
problem solve. Activities such
as crying or eating before
you solve a problem are
responses of the Spontaneous
and Adaptive or the feeling
part of the personality. We
will talk about that next
week.*

Say: *Giving information, solving
problems, estimating
probability, and gathering
and considering data are all
functions of the Problem
Solving Part. Opinions and
beliefs are expressed from
the Nurturing and
Structuring Part.*

Part two:

Put a chalk mark or a strip of
masking tape down the center of
the room. Place the **Nurturing and
Structuring Part** marker on one
side and the **Problem Solving Part**
marker on the other.

Say: *I will read six statements. If
you think a statement is
probably from the Nurturing
and Structuring Part, stand*
*on the Nurturing and
Structuring Part side of the
line. If you think it is from
the Problem Solving Part,
stand on the Problem Solving
Part side.*

Ask: *Will you do that now?*

Say: 1. *"I think that you should
run faster." (Nurturing and
Structuring Part opinion)*

2. *"I timed you, and you ran
a kilometer in five
minutes." (Problem
Solving Part data-
collecting statement)*

3. *"Will you tell me your
opinion about smoking?"
(Problem Solving Part data
gathering)*

4. *"I have listed the values
held by people that I think
will affect the decision
about where to place the
airport." (Problem Solving
Part data collecting and
evaluation)*

5. *"Here are four things that I
believe should be done
about drug abuse."
(Nurturing and Structuring
Part opinion)*

6. *"I think the third one
would probably be most
effective with an alcoholic
friend." (Problem Solving
Part probability
estimation)*

Part three:

Hand out copies of the **Problem
Solving Part** sheet, Meeting 4,
page 131.

Say: *Item seven, on
contamination, refers to*

using unexamined Nurturing and Structuring Part opinions or prejudices or Spontaneous and Adaptive Part wishes as if they were factual data. An example of this is: "Since young people are unreliable, we will hire someone over twenty-one for this job." That is Nurturing and Structuring Part opinion contamination. Some young people are reliable. "Families must get along well" is Spontaneous or Adaptive wish contamination. Some families do not get along well, and yet the people in them still grow and are healthy.

Ask: *Will you read the rest of the sheet at home?*

Say: *In order to have high self-esteem, people need to be able to solve problems. That requires a strong Problem Solving Part.*

Hand out copies of **How to Strengthen the Problem Solving Part,** Meeting 4, page 132.

Ask: *Will you take this home and read it and do at least one activity to strengthen your Problem Solving Part?*

Ask: *Will you turn to pages 106 and 107 in the text, called What You Stroke is What You Get, and at the top write the name of someone who is important to you?*
In the top box write about a time when he nurtured and structured well.

In the center box write about a problem he solved.
Before the next meeting, tell him about what you noticed.

Say: *Using the Suggestion Circle is one way we strengthen our thinking ability during these meetings.*

If you did not do a Suggestion Circle right after goal setting, do one now. Use a topic that someone asked for during goal setting or do a circle on "How can I encourage my child to think clearly?" (Identify the age of the child, eighteen months or older.)

Part four:

Say: **Centering**[2] *is listed on the handout sheet, Ways to Strengthen the Problem Solving Part (item 13).*

Ask: *How many of you already practice Centering?*
Will you help the rest of us get Centered?

Ask: *Will the person who took the survey at the last meeting stand on the Problem Solving Part marker in the posture you use when you are taking a survey? This is a Problem Solving Part activity. Will the rest of you describe his posture and expression? (Head, shoulders, and hips level, body straight, face and voice serious or purposeful.)*

Stand centered.

Say: *It takes less energy to hold the body upright when its center of gravity is in line*

121

with the pull of the earth's gravity.

Stand off center.

Say: *More energy is expended when one's body is opposing gravity, or uncentered. Using more energy to hold up the body leaves less energy for thinking clearly. Centering helps people to be potent without confusion. There is stability in being centered.*

Ask: *Will you stand with your feet flat on the floor, slightly apart, and think of your feet as roots planted firmly in the ground?*

Say: *This contributes to the feeling of being "in the here and now"—a kind of alertness that differs from recalling the past or anticipating the future.*

Ask: *Will you breathe deeply several times? As you do, imagine your body being lifted by a golden cord attached to the top of your head, toward the back. Do not stick your chin out. Do not lock your knees, as this stops the positive flow of energy.*

Say: *Imagine a plumb line through the center of your body, and stand centered around the plumb line. People who have been standing uncentered for a long time may feel awkward or uncomfortable, until they practice being centered for a few days.*

Ask: *Will you check each other to see that your weight is evenly distributed from front to back and side to side?*

Ask: *Will you choose a partner and follow these three directions?*
   1. *Stand uncentered, say "No!" and think about how that feels.*
   2. *Stand centered, say "No!" and think about how that feels.*
   3. *Ask your partner if the "No!" sounded different from the centered and uncentered positions.*

Ask: *Will you do that now?*

After about two minutes . . .

Ask: *Will you share your thoughts and feelings about being centered and uncentered?*

Ask: *Will you practice centering at least three times between now and the next meeting?*

Reassemble people in a circle.

2. AFFIRMATIONS FOR THINKING
(15 Minutes)

Ask: *Will anyone share thoughts, feelings, or opinions about the affirmations we have been practicing? Did anyone discover a new way to use the affirmations?*

Ask: *Will someone report on how you used Affirmations for Being, page 49 in the text, or for Structure, page 173?*

Point to the **Affirmations for Thinking** poster.

Ask: *Will you read the **Thinking Affirmations** with me?*

AFFIRMATIONS FOR THINKING
I'm glad you are growing up.
You can let people know when you feel angry.
You can think about your feelings, and you can feel about your thinking.
You can think for yourself; you don't have to take care of other people by thinking for them.
You don't have to be uncertain; you can be sure about what you need.

Hand out a set of **Affirmations for Thinking** cymbals to each person.

Ask: *Will you pick out one or two you would most like to hear? Would you rather hear the anger affirmation stated as it is on the poster or as it is in the text on page 111?*

Say: *These are the Affirmations for Thinking. They are important for children eighteen months to three years old, for young people in the middle teens, and for everyone who wants to do cause-and-effect thinking. These messages focus on thinking and feeling. They counter cultural messages that invite boys to think and girls to be dependent or confused.*

Say: *This **visualization** is a personal one.*

Ask: *Will you close your eyes and visualize yourself as the competent thinker that you are capable of being? Listen to these affirmations and see if any of them is helpful to you today.*

Read the affirmations "To an adult" on page 112 of the text or write your own especially for this group.

Ask: *Did the ones you liked best in that reading correspond to the cymbals you picked out earlier?*

3. RESPONSIBILITY
(15-20 Minutes)

Ask: *Will someone who practiced asking direct questions instead of saying "Your eggs are getting cold" tell how you did that? Will someone who indicated that people, not things, are responsible for behavior—"Things are falling into place"—tell how you did that?*

Say: *One of the Thinking Affirmations, "You don't have to take care of me by thinking for me," is the key to the third exercise on **responsibility.** It is called Eat Your Beans for Mommy and focuses on communications that invite young children to begin to be responsible for themselves rather than for adults. The skills practiced in this* *exercise are also helpful to adults who are encouraging teenagers to separate in straightforward ways.*

Say: *The Eat Your Beans for Mommy/Take Care of Me exercise allows us to experience ways in which adults, without meaning to, invite children to think for the adults or to feel responsible for them. It will give us a chance to find ways to say, "You don't have to take care of me by thinking for me."*

Ask: *Will each of you find a partner? Will one of you sit on the floor and listen while the other stands and reads the statement on one of these cards? Think how you would feel if you were a young child hearing that statement. Together, rewrite the messages in such a way that they give the child information or ask the child to take responsibility for himself without implying that he is responsible for the adult's feelings.*

Hand each person one 3x5 card on which one of the following messages is written:
1. Eat your beans for Mommy. (age 3)
2. You make me so very, verrry happy! (age 2)
3. Drink your milk for Daddy. (age 2)
4. Joshua, your Daddy looks tired. Be very quiet all evening, and don't get on his nerves. (age 3)
5. Do it in the pot for Mommy. (age 2½)
6. You drive me insane. (age 3)
7. Be nice for Grandma, or she won't think I'm a good mother. (age 3)
8. I am going on a business trip, John, you take good care of Mommy while I'm gone. (age 4)
9. Be quiet. You'll give me a migraine headache. (age 3)
10. I am going to see Grandpa. You take good care of Daddy while I'm gone. (age 4)
11. Karla, you know how angry your dad gets if you kids squabble. Don't tease! (age 2)
12. Janie, I had you to make me happy. (age 2)
13. If you ever did anything like that, it would kill me. (age 3½)
14. Jimmy, don't climb around like that, you'll give me a heart attack. (age 19 months)
15. We were going to get a divorce. We had you to keep us together.

After four or five minutes . . .

Ask: *Will you come together as a group now? Will you read the words on your card, tell how you felt about the message, and then read the way you rewrote it?*
EXAMPLES of rewritten statements that encourage children to be responsible for themselves:
1. Eat your beans.
2. I am happy when I am with you.
3. Drink your milk.
4. Here is Daddy!
5. Pee in the pot, not on the floor.

124

6. I need five minutes of quiet.
7. I will be glad to see Grandma, will you?
8. I'm going on a business trip, John. Mommy will take care of you while I am away.
9. Kendyll, find a quiet game for awhile. My head hurts, and I need some quiet time. You can pretend you are sailing in a big sailboat.
10. I am going to see Grandpa. Daddy will take care of you while I am gone.
11. Karla, you are getting to be very good at arguing.
12. Janie, I love you.
13. I do not like that person's behavior.
14. Jimmy, climb here, not there.
15. Sometimes your mom and I have problems, but they are our problems, not yours.

Say: *Remember, the affirmation "You don't have to take care of me by thinking for me" is intended to mean: "Little people don't have to be responsible for big people." It also means: "Adults don't have to be responsible for each other's feelings or try to know what people want without asking." Adults are, however, responsible for thinking for infants and for using cause-and-effect thinking about how their behavior affects other people.*

Say: *Turn to the Affirmations for Thinking on pages 110, 111, and 112 in the text.*

Ask: *Will you follow the directions on page 111 and write these affirmations for someone else and for yourself? Will you practice getting and giving the ones you believe before the next meeting?*

Say: *You can think of ingenious ways to give these affirmations to yourself. You can tape all of the affirmations you need to hear and listen to the cassette tape player often.*

___

OPTIONAL:

4. PARENTING TIPS
(5-20 Minutes)

Ask: *Does anyone have any thoughts or questions to share about the Parenting Tips on pages 102 and 103 in the text? or about Chapter four?*

✳

Use the discussion questions on How to Handle Two Year Olds When They Yell, Kick and Scream[3]
- as a handout
- as a group discussion, item by item
- by dividing the group into clusters of three or four persons to choose and discuss three items
- by assigning two or three items to each cluster to discuss and report back to the whole group

5. STROKE BANK THEORY[4] *(5-10 Minutes)*

Ask: *Will someone review what a stroke is? If anyone did the* ✻ *Jelly Bean exercise at home, will you tell how you used it?*

Say: *The Stroke Bank Theory, pages 95-97 in the text, is an analogy that compares the amount of money reflected by a bank balance to the level of strokes one registers in one's feeling capacity. It assumes that people are responsible for their own stroke level. We will discuss the theory and think about how full our banks are today.*

Post the **Stroke Bank** poster.

Say: *Jim's Stroke Bank is the size that will hold an optimum amount of strokes for him. People's banks may be different sizes—two bushels, a ton, four kilograms—no matter, each person's bank will hold the amount he needs.*

Invite people to describe the different levels depicted on page 109 in the text and on the Stroke Bank poster.

or . . .

Point to and describe each level.

1. Empty—Jim is dead.
2. 0-20% filled is very low! People whose stroke banks are that low are usually institutionalized. Jim is in a hospital or prison.
3. 20-66⅔%—Jim is just living—getting along, surviving another day. "Thank goodness it's Friday." or "Oh, yuk, Monday again!" Jim needs strokes and will grab almost any stroke that is offered. Plastics are better than none.
4. 66⅔-87½% is good living—Jim feels really great. He looks for positive strokes and may reject destructive ones.
5. 87½-100% is Jim's safety deposit box area. His stroke bank is so full he can store some strokes for future use. His well-being and vitality attract positive strokes, and he is comfortable rejecting negative strokes. Hedges Capers says this is why the rich get richer and the poor get poorer.

Ask each person:
Where is your Stroke Bank level right now?

Say: *It is possible to give strokes when one's bank is at any level. These are the questions for us to think about:*
1. *Do I give different strokes when my level is at seventy-five than I do when it is at forty?*
2. *Where must my level be for me to give positive strokes freely?*
3. *Do I feel differently about giving strokes to others when my level is low than when it is high?*

Ask: *Each of us is responsible for our own stroke level—getting and keeping good ones. Do any of you want to raise your Stroke Bank level by*

126

asking for some strokes right now?

Encourage the people who said "yes" to do so.

Ask: *At what age can parents start teaching children to take some responsibility for their own stroke levels? Six months? Three years? Six years?*

Say: *We will talk more about the Stroke Bank exercise on page 109 after we discuss stroke rules.*

6. DISCOUNTING
(5 Minutes)

Say: *One way in which people lower the quality and number of good feeling strokes is by the process of discounting. Let's think about what discounting is.*

Ask: *If you buy an electrical appliance that has been discounted, what might be the facts about that item?*
EXAMPLE:
a bargain
out of style
discontinued
damaged
no one else wants it

Say: *Buying something you want at a discount price may be positive. To discount something psychologically, to make it less in some way, is negative. There are three areas that people discount.*

Write on board or on newsprint with felt pen.

| 1. Other persons |
| 2. Oneself |
| 3. The situation |

Ask: *Will someone identify which of the following situations discount others, self, or the situation? All discounts ultimately discount self.*
  1. *There is much thunder and lightning, and I continue to play golf.* (situation and self)
  2. *My kids are out of control and there is nothing I can do.* (self)
  3. *My boss is so closed minded, there is no point in telling him my ideas.* (other and self)
  4. *I can't accept a compliment unless I am positive the person who gave it is sincere.* (other and self)
  5. *I don't need strokes—I'm tough.* (self)
  6. *There aren't many good strokes in my life right now, but there is nothing I can do about it.* (self)

Say: *Watch for examples of discounting while we examine stroke rules.*

7. STROKE RULES
(20-30 Minutes)

Hand out list of **Stroke Rules** compiled from last meeting.

Ask: *Will you keep in mind the following items as we*

examine the list of stroke rules.

1. *Each of us needs strokes every day in order to live.*
2. *Each of us needs rules by which to run our lives. These rules are part of our Nurturing and Structuring Part. Our rules are our own responsibility, and if they aren't working for us, it is our job to change them.*
3. *Stroke Rules can protect and fill our Stroke Banks or they can discount strokes—reduce the number and quality of strokes that we collect.*

Ask: *Will each person revise five rules?*

Assign five rules to each person. *Will you star the statements you agree with, cross out or rewrite the rest, and add any new ones that you think of?* EXAMPLES: pages 78-79 in text.

Divide people into groups of three or four to share and discuss their revised lists for five or six minutes.

Say: *People need not agree. The purpose of the exercise is to update our own Nurturing and Structuring Part tapes, not to install someone else's in place of the tape we already have. Please honor and respect each person's position rather than urging people to change.*

Reassemble the group.

Ask: *Will each small group share one item with the large group?*

OPTIONAL:
If the group is small and the list is short (twenty items), read each rule and ask someone to tell whether she kept that rule or rewrote it, and how she rewrote it?

Say: *Each of our stroke rules originally had some functional purpose, maybe when we were very young. Rules that once helped us stay alive will no longer help us if, in our present life situation, they discount ourselves, others, or the situation.*

Read aloud page 80 in the text or ask someone to tell what it means to him. Invite people to make notes to themselves on the page.

Ask: *Will you fill in the Stroke Bank sheet found in the text, page 109, and bring it to the next meeting? There are examples on page 108.*

OPTIONAL:
Show your mobile. Add a paper tab to one person and observe the movement. Add a paper clip to another person and observe the movement.

Say: *Perhaps some of you would like to make a mobile of your family to watch it flutter gently or bounce violently. Think about what rules help your family adjust to change and what new rules might be helpful to your family.*

128

Ask: *Will you think about discounting again? Walter wants to change a Stroke Rule from "All strokes must be earned" to "Give Doing strokes that are earned and give free strokes for Being." He starts telling his kids that he likes them and they are important to him. He hasn't done much of this and he sounds awkward and unsure of himself. His children say, "Hey, Dad, weird . . . what are you doing? We don't believe that junk. You sick or something?"*

Ask: *Will four people volunteer to read one of Walter's four possible responses?*

Hand out cards with **four possible responses** Walter might make.

Ask: *Will the group identify whether the response discounts self, other, or situation?*

Have people read the cards in any order.

1. I'll stop. I'm too old to change. They are probably right.
2. I'll stop. It's too hard for me to change, and it would be too confusing to my kids.
3. I'll continue. I'm not doing too well, but I will give it more time. They may decide they like it.
4. I'll continue. I'm going to do this because it is good for me. They can like it or lump it.

Ask: *Does anyone have another response that Walter could have given? Does it discount self, other, or situation?*

If the group has not done a Four Ways of Parenting exercise earlier in the meeting, do one of someone's choice, or turn to page 105 in the text and do the one on changing the Nurturing and Structuring Part about toilet training. Refer to Meeting 3, page 99 for directions.

8. ADDITIONS

Address any items added during goal setting.

CLOSING (5 Minutes)

Point to the **Goal** poster and note the content covered. Take care of any business details.

Say: *These are your homework activities for the next meeting.*
   1. *Read the Problem Solving Part sheet and the Ways to Strengthen the Problem Solving Part.*
   2. *Practice Centering and observe whether and how you think differently when you are centered.*
   3. *Do the worksheet on page 107 in the text and reinforce someone's ability to think.*
   4. *Practice the Thinking Affirmations on yourself and someone else, page 111 in text.*

5. *Answer the How to Handle Two Year Olds When They Yell, Kick, and Scream.* (Optional)
6. *Do the Stroke Bank exercise on page 109 in the text.*
7. *Think of ways to encourage your children to be responsible for their own stroke levels.*
8. *Make a family mobile.* (Optional)
9. *Read Chapter three through page 80 and pages 257, 258.*

Ask: *Does anyone have any Resentments? Appreciations?*

Ask: *On the way out will each of you tell two people something you especially appreciate about them?*

Say: *Thank you. The meeting is closed. I'll see you next meeting.*

Our Problem Solving Part

When we are using the Problem Solving Part of us:

1. We gather data.
   We ask other people for information and look things up in reference books.
2. We compute.
   We use multiplication tables, charts, and graphs.
3. We estimate probability.
   "Dark clouds, gusty wind, temperature dropping, I'll probably get wet before I get home unless I get a ride."
4. We solve problems in the here and now.
   "How's the weather look for a picnic?" "Dark clouds look like rain." (The Structuring Part of us solves problems by old rules: "Red sky at night, Sailors delight, Red sky in morning, Sailors take warning." The Adaptive Part of us solves problems out of early feelings. "Of course it will rain—it *always* rains when I plan a picnic."
5. The Problem Solving Part of us is positive if it is appropriately used. It is appropriate if there are problems to be solved, old ideas to be examined and up-dated, data to be collected.
6. It is inappropriate if the Problem Solving Part is used instead of having fun, nurturing, or grieving. "Here we are at a party having fun, and all she wants to do is discuss the implications of the data collected in the latest experiment with monkeys!"
7. It does not function well if it is contaminated with prejudices and delusions.
8. Human beings from eighteen months to three years of age are busy starting the Problem Solving Part of their personalities. It can be strengthened and sharpened for the rest of their lives.

How to Strengthen the Problem Solving Part of Your Personality

1. Do arithmetic.
2. Fit a pattern.
3. Work a puzzle.
4. Build something.
5. Take a survey.
6. Do a comparison.
7. Sort Parts of the Personality—what do I think I should do, what do I want to do, what is most apt to work?
8. Say the Affirmations for Thinking.
9. Do scientific thinking: define a problem; collect pertinent data; decide what is most likely to work; do it; evaluate the results.
10. Stroke clear thinking.
11. Paraphrase: listen to what someone says; think about what he said; use your own words to report back to him what you think he meant; continue until he says, "Yes, that is what I mean."
12. Spend time thinking with other good thinkers.
13. Practice Centering.
14. Examine a prejudice and replace it with facts.
15.
16.

Discussion Questions:
How To Handle Two Year Olds
When They Yell, Kick, and Scream

Sometime between the ages of eighteen months and three years most children do part of their developmental task of separating from their parents and expanding their own thinking powers by trying out some very loud, active behavior. This may be treated in a casual, routine manner, or it may be given a label, usually "tantrum," and treated as if it were a problem. The following questions were assembled by a group of parents to help them talk through and think through their own beliefs and feelings about responding to angry-acting two year olds.

1. How do we let a child know that anger is OK but that he is not to damage property, hurt people, or hurt himself?
2. What is the developmental task of the two year old that seems to trigger a higher level of frustration than he may have displayed at other ages?
3. What do we do if the child is having a "tantrum"? (The dictionary says a tantrum is "a violent demonstration of rage or frustration. . . .")
4. How were we feeling before, after, and during "the tantrum"?
5. Are a two year old's "tantrums" a way of finding out "Who's in charge around here"?
6. Is it OK to be mad at brothers and sisters but not at Mom and Dad?
7. If we hit the child to make him stop when he's having a "tantrum," are we teaching him that "big people" can hit?
8. If we have men do the corporal punishment, do children learn early that boys can hit but girls cannot?
9. Does the threat of "wait till your dad gets home" role model male violence?
10. Are crying and screaming OK at home?, at the store?, at Grandma's?, or in public places?
11. To what extent do we ask kids to "take care of Mommy and Daddy" if we ask them to be nice all the time?
12. Is there something you need to help you feel more comfortable while you live with people who are two years old and noisy?

Homework

1. Read Problem Solving Part sheet and Ways to Strengthen the Problem Solving Part of Your Personality.
2. Practice Centering and observe how you think differently when you are centered.
3. Do the worksheet on page 107 in the text and reinforce someone's ability to think.
4. Practice the Thinking Affirmations on yourself and someone else, page 111 in text.
5. Answer the How to Handle Two Year Olds When They Yell, Kick, and Scream discussion questions. (Optional)
6. Do the Stroke Bank exercise on page 109 in the text.
7. Think of ways to encourage your children to be responsible for their own stroke levels.
8. Make a family mobile. (Optional)
9. Read Chapter three through page 80 and pages 257 and 258.

Notes

1. Jean Illsley Clarke, "The Terrific Twos," *Child Care Resources* (Mound, Minn.: Quality Child Care Press, Inc., 1980).
2. Thanks to Jean Madgett for her suggestions on Centering.
3. Thanks to Jean Koski for developing the list of discussion questions, How to Handle Two Year Olds When They Yell, Kick, and Scream.
4. Hedges Capers and Glen Holland, "Stroke Survival Quotient," *Transactional Analysis Journal* vol. 1, no. 3. This article describes the theory which Capers later called the Stroke Bank Theory.

LETTER TO MARJ 5

Dear Marj,
This fifth lesson reminds me of a class that Kathy Westgard, Dottie Tompson, and I taught at a Chemical Abuse Prevention Center. And I mean "taught," not "led." At each meeting we offered the right to pass and everyone took it. Anyone want to share? No. Anyone willing to tell? No. Anything to add? No. I was thankful to have a team teacher and an apprentice. We went ahead. We did the exercises. We did Suggestion Circles of three. We played all the roles in the Four Ways of Parenting. And we did *not* know what was going on. They came. They watched. They left. On the fifth night, at the beginning of the meeting, one of the women said, "I know you have your things ready to show us, but is it all right if I tell what has been happening at home first?" All right indeed. She told how she had been changing her way of nurturing and of asking for what she wanted. Other people told similar stories. When we asked why they hadn't talked before, they told us they were not ready to. They were hungry for alternative ways of parenting, and they didn't want to interrupt. Once they decided that we weren't going to judge them, that we were improving our parenting too, they took off! Suddenly they were doing about eighty percent of the work, and Kathy and Dottie and I were doing a supportive twenty percent. This was exciting and an important lesson for me—trust the group—when they are ready to take over, they will.

About the content of Meeting 5: The whispering of secrets introduces the Spontaneous and Adaptive Part of the Personality. Often the energy level of the group rises remarkably during this name tag opener.

Ground Rules are still important!

1. Listen carefully and note any changes in **Personal Goals** for review at the eighth meeting. One father said, "I came to improve the self-esteem of my boys. Now I realize that I have to make some changes in myself as well. I'm using fewer Plastics and starting to ask straighter questions."

2. Follow the **Stroke Quotient Decision Theory** *exactly!* Move rapidly so people will not have time to think up reasonable discounts. This is the most important part of Meeting 5, and it is the final step for many people in accepting responsibility for their own stroke economy. To some people it makes sense, and they like it. To others it makes sense, and they resist it. Mary said, "Yes, but, does it work?" I asked if she had a number in mind for her own stroke quotient. "Yes." "Is it like either of your

list numbers?" "The same." "Does this number correspond to the strokes you got yesterday?" "Yes, but I still don't believe it." "OK." Our job is to present. To invite.

3. Centering is a potent way to **Reject Toxic Strokes** for some people. Judy Howard is excited about centering because she says she can think more clearly when she is centered. A friend of hers doesn't like centering. She doesn't believe it helps her and doesn't practice it. As far as I can see, those two people are both living happily ever after. We offer options. People decide what they need and will use.

4. The very important activities for the **Spontaneous and Adaptive Part** of our personality are the most *fun* to do of any of the Three Parts of the Personality exercises! Encouraging people to care for and enjoy their feeling part is important because it adds enjoyment and excitement to life. I like to do the whole exercise, but if you have done several Four Parents and have to compress something, include at least the Aunt Mable exercise. It demonstrates clearly the Four Ways of Responding from the Spontaneous and Adaptive Part of our personality. When I have problems teaching about the Spontaneous and Adaptive Part of us, they are usually reflections of one of the following three misconceptions:

● that the Spontaneous Part is all free and fun, whee, zip, wow! and that there is no sad or angry or gloomy side

● that adaptiveness is only obedient compliance. The rebellious "I won't do it because she wants me to" is also adaptive. It is acting in response to the other person's stimuli in a formula way

● that the feeling part is childish and not suitable for grown people.

The interview helps confront all three of these misinterpretations because it encourages each person to discover that she does function in different spontaneous and adaptive ways. The balloon play and fantasy trip reinforce those discoveries.

I advise you to talk fast during the information-giving part of this section to give people adequate time to do the role play. This is advisable because the Spontaneous and Adaptive Part in people is intolerant of long lectures and is anxious to explore and try things out. People who want to talk instead of play can "pass," but don't let them drag other people into long intellectual discussions about the Spontaneous and Adaptive Part during the meeting

You probably have lots of good Spontaneous and Adaptive Part activities to recommend in your part of the country and many

138

good readings. A nice skinny book that helped me remember about "wonder" is Clyde Reid's *Celebrate the Temporary*.[1]

5. Your group probably will be skillful at doing the **Four Ways of Parenting** exercise by now. If a simple one is taking longer than five minutes, go back to Meeting 3, page 99, and review the steps. Or make a tape recording of a meeting (with the permission of the group) and listen to your technique to discover how you can make the exercise crisper.

   People probably have recognized by now that the Marshmallowing and Criticizing ways of parenting consistently discount the other person, the situation, and ultimately one's self.

6. **Separating Sex and Nurturing** is a powerful idea. Many women have been taught to nurture, and many men have been taught that nurturing is not masculine but sex is. The pact helps people to try new behavior for a very short time. It does not demand that they change their approach or life-style. It doesn't matter that they feel uncomfortable or awkward. I know couples who declare that they have used this idea to improve their relationships by raising the level of satisfying nurturing and satisfying sex in their lives.

7. The **Affirmations for Doing** are special to me. When my oldest son was little he didn't want to try new things because he couldn't do them well.

   We gave him a lot of strokes for doing cute things and didn't think about how demanding that could be. I wish I had known then how to talk about what he was doing and to keep that separate from accepting him as a person (Being) while he learned new skills.

8. You Are Going to Love This is one more step in the journey of identifying who is responsible for what. I like the way people groan, mutter something about having said that very thing yesterday, shake their heads, and then plunge into these **Responsibility** exercises with energy and excitement. Keep it brisk. I believe that people learn more from a few minutes of laughing at themselves and practicing responsible language each week than from an hour's serious discussion about the importance of encouraging responsibility in children.

9. **Tips for Parenting** the six to eighteen month old is an optional exercise. Ah, yes, permission, permission, permission! Give yourself permission to see the young explorer as an explorer. And permission to the caring adults to take good care of themselves so they can enjoy the explorations rather than experiencing the resulting disorder as an intrusion into an orderly world.

Do end on time. The **Closing** suggests singing "London Bridge Is Falling Down." I was scared to try it, but after all the kid activities in this meeting, my groups sing it with gusto and fall down and giggle. Good feeling strokes. You may have a Spontaneous and Adaptive Part stroke activity you would rather use.

Resentments and Appreciations are information—do not defend and do not blame. I hope people are giving them freely by now.

I love you a bushel and a peck!

Jean

MEETING 5

BEFORE MEETING 5

1. Study Meeting 5 plan.
2. Reread Chapter three in text, pages 257, 258, and 263.
3. Read the fifth Letter to Marj.
4. Review personal goals (why people came) obtained from Meeting 1.
5. Reread "Who, Me, Lead a Group?", Question 2, Step 5.
6. Collect the following **supplies:**
   paper for name tags
   felt pens or crayons
   tape or pins
   half sheets of paper
   balloons
   masking tape
   chalkboard or newsprint
7. Make or collect the following **visual aids:**

POSTERS
- Goals for Meeting 5, page 142
- Ground Rules, Meeting 1, page 37
- All six Affirmation posters, Meeting 2, page 63

CARDS AND SIGNS
- Cards for You Are Going to Love This, Meeting 5, page 153
- List of adjectives for Stroke Quotient exercise, Meeting 5, page 143
- Four one-word signs reading: "Free," "Ingenious," "Compliant," "Rebellious," Meeting 5, page 147
- Affirmation for Doing cymbals, Marj 2, page 58

DUPLICATED HANDOUTS
- Spontaneous and Adaptive Part of the Personality, Meeting 5, page 156
- Responses from the Spontaneous and Adaptive Part, Meeting 5, page 158
- How to Strengthen Your Spontaneous and Adaptive Part, Meeting 5, page 160
- Time Out for Nurturing, Meeting 5, page 161
- Homework, Meeting 5, page 162

OPENING (5 Minutes)

Post the posters.

NAMES

Pass out name tags and pens.

Ask: *Will you make a name tag for a partner?*
Will you put the name tag on her and whisper a silly secret in her ear? Will you introduce your partner and tell one reason you like her, (but not tell the secret)?

GROUND RULES

Ask: *Will someone identify all five Ground Rules? If you have identified a Ground Rule that you wish were used in another group, will you tell us which rule it is?*

Refer to the **Ground Rules** poster, Meeting 1, page 37.

GOALS

Point to the **Goals** poster.

```
MEETING 5 GOALS
 1. Personal Goals
 2. Stroke Quotient
    Theory
 3. Rejecting
    Destructive Strokes
 4. Spontaneous and
    Adaptive Part of the
    Personality
 5. Four Ways of
    Parenting
 6. Separating Sex and
    Nurturing
 7. Affirmations for
    Doing
 8. Responsibility
 9. Parenting Tips
10. Additions
11. Celebrations
```

Read and negotiate the Goals.

1. *Personal Goals* —We will review our personal goals.
2. *Stroke Quotient Decision Theory*—We will consider the theory and how rules about stroking relate to it.
3. *Rejecting Destructive Strokes* —We will practice using Centering to help us reject destructive strokes.
4. *Spontaneous and Adaptive Part* —We will learn why this part is important and how to take care of it.

5. *Four Ways of Parenting* —We will do the Four Parent exercise.
6. *Separating Sex and Nurturing* —We will learn what a Separating Sex and Nurturing pact is and how it is important.
7. *Affirmations for Doing* —We will practice some.
8. *Responsibility* —This exercise shows how to encourage children to be responsible for their own thoughts and feelings. It is called *You Are Going to Love This.*
9. *Parenting Tips* —Does anyone want time to discuss Parenting Tips for six to eighteen month olds?
10. *Additions*—Does anyone have suggestions for topics to be addressed by a Suggestion Circle or a Four Parent?
11. *Celebrations*—Does anyone want to share a celebration or an awareness from the past week? (Do so now.)

1. REVIEW OF PERSONAL GOALS
(10-20 Minutes)

Using the personal goals record you made at the first meeting, interview each class member to see if she is experiencing what she wanted for herself. Use the Four Ways of Parenting or the Suggestion Circle for specific problems if that seems appropriate. Take notes on any new goals.

2. STROKE QUOTIENT DECISION THEORY

(15-20 Minutes)

Say: *We will be talking about strokes and the Stroke Quotient Decision Theory.*

Ask: *Will each of you say what your Stroke Bank level was when you entered the room today? Refer to page 109 in the text if you need to refresh your memory.*

Ask: *Does anyone want to raise her level right now by getting some strokes?*

If so, let her ask for what she wants. Invite her to ask the group, make a phone call, or do whatever she needs to do to get the good strokes she wants.

Say: *Today we will consider the Stroke Quotient Decision Theory that you read about on pages 57 and 58 in the text. This is a theory which suggests that people decide what proportion of positive and negative strokes they deserve or will register and that they will seek out those strokes, either deliberately or outside of awareness. We will use lists of adjectives to explore this theory. Do not show your lists to anybody else. They are personal and private.*

Read these directions step by step.

Ask: *Will you turn to page 81 in your text? Number one to ten and list ten adjectives, descriptive words, positive or negative, that describe you.*

Say: *Put a plus or a minus beside each word—plus if this is a positive thing in your life and minus if it is negative.*

Say: *Add the number of pluses.*

Ask: *Will you turn to the back inside cover of your book and number from one to ten?*

Say: *I will read ten words. Beside each number put a plus if the word describes you and a minus if it does not describe you.*

Read a list of ten positive adjectives that you believe apply to the whole group.

EXAMPLES:
intelligent, good looking, caring, persistent, energetic, growing, loving, courageous, forward looking, exciting, fun, friendly, prompt, pleasant, thoughtful, supportive, challenging

Say: *Add the number of pluses. Put your book aside and listen to the theory. We will return to the lists later.*

Ask: *Will someone explain the Stroke Quotient Decision Theory?*

OPTIONAL:
Read aloud the Stroke Quotient Decision Theory on pages 57 and 58 in text.

Ask: *Does this theory sound true?*

Say: *Here are some questions for you to think about.*

Read the questions slowly.
- *Does this theory explain someone's behavior to you?*
- *Could it explain why some men (without being conscious of it) look for +70 and -30 wives?*
- *Could it be why some wives stay with husbands who batter?*
- *Could it be why some people criticize themselves?*
- *Could it explain why you hear some channels louder than others on the Four Ways of Parenting exercise?*

Ask: *Does anyone want to comment on any of these questions?*

Ask: *Will you guess what your own Stroke Quotient might be and write it on the back inside cover of your book? For how many of you are the scores on your two lists within two or three points of each other?*

Ask: *For how many of you is the quotient you guessed close to the numbers on your lists? Do you know that the list of ten words that I read describe all of you in my opinion?*

Say: *I would give each of you plus ten on the list. If you gave yourself less, try to decide why. Is it because I don't see you accurately, or is it because you made the list fit your stroke quotient?*

Say: *If this theory fits for me, if I decided on a daily quota of positive and negative strokes, I can decide to change those numbers. If my quotient was +70 and -30 I can move to +75 and -25. My family may try to pull me back to my old ways just because familiar ways are comfortable, even if they are partly negative.*

Say: *If the theory makes sense to you, pause for a moment and say some words of appreciation to yourself for finding a quota that would help you when you need it, even if it doesn't make sense for you now. Try, "I'm glad I decided to get enough strokes to live," or "I'm glad I found a way to make sense of my world," or "I was a smart kid to figure that out."*

Say: *One way a person can maintain a certain stroke quotient is with stroke rules. Look at the rules you wrote on page 109 in the text.*

Ask: *Does one of those rules fit with your stroke quotient? Does anyone recall a rule from the Stroke Rules that would help a person maintain a high stroke quotient? Does anyone recall a rule that would help a person discount positive strokes in order to maintain a low stroke quotient?*

Say: *If you want to change some rules you can start changing behavior a bit right today.*

144

OPTIONAL:

Ask: Did anyone construct a family mobile? If you brought it along, will you show it? What did you observe about its balance?

Say: The Systems Theory, as demonstrated by the mobile and Stroke Quotient Theory, explains why you can, by repeatedly changing a little bit at a time, make a big change in stroke patterns without throwing a family into turmoil.

3. REJECTING DESTRUCTIVE STROKES *(5-10 Minutes)*

Say: *Today we will practice Centering again and we will experiment with rejecting destructive strokes from a centered position.*

Ask: *Who practiced Centering this week? Any change in communication patterns?*

Say: *Destructive strokes tear down self-esteem. Plastics and Don't be messages are examples of negative or destructive strokes.*

Ask: *Will you choose one of these examples or a similar stroke that you would like to throw away?*
EXAMPLES:
1. You did a lousy job, you no good thing.

2. If it weren't for you I would be happy.
3. You are dumb.
4. You don't belong in this group.

Ask: *Will you choose a partner and ask her to say the destructive stroke to you twice? Listen first uncentered and say, "I don't accept that." Listen the second time centered and say, "I don't accept that." Do not explain or apologize. Reverse roles.*

Reassemble the group.

Ask: *Which did you prefer— centered or uncentered? Will you practice this exercise for homework?*

Say: *Remember: Destructive strokes lower self-esteem. Negative messages that we need to hear may feel unpleasant, but they are not destructive; they are constructive, and in the long run they raise self-esteem.*

Ask: *Anyone want to share ways in which you encouraged your children to be responsible for their own stroke levels? Did any of you teach your children to center?*

Say: *We can use our Problem Solving Parts to decide whether strokes are destructive or constructive.*

Ask: *Does anyone have questions or comments on the Problem Solving Part sheet you took home to read? Did any of*

145

*you do something to
strengthen your Problem
Solving Part this week?*

4. SPONTANEOUS AND ADAPTIVE PART OF THE PERSONALITY
(10-30 Minutes)

Say: *People with high self-esteem
have healthy, happy
Spontaneous and Adaptive
Parts. This section explains
what the Spontaneous and
Adaptive Part is and suggests
ways to strengthen it. Ways
in which a person complies
or rebels through the
Spontaneous and Adaptive
Part will be demonstrated.*

Ask: *Will two or three people tell:*
  - *something they do that's
  fun.*
  - *something that they do
  regularly that they don't
  especially like doing.*
  - *something that they should
  do but rebel against and
  won't do.*
  - *some ways that they get
  out of doing things they are
  supposed to do.*

List these items on the board or
newsprint in four columns titled:

FUN	DON'T WANT TO DO
(Free)	(Compliant)

WON'T DO	TRICKS
(Rebellious)	(Ingenious)

Say: *We are going to observe and
experience the Spontaneous
and Adaptive Part in action.*

Toss out balloons.
Blow yours and play with it.
Encourage others to do the same.
After some play and laughter . . .

Say: *Will you go on a fantasy trip
to find out about some other
facet of your Spontaneous
and Adaptive Part? I will
guide you on the trip and
you can come back at any
time. Sit comfortably, close
your eyes, breathe deeply.
Hold your balloon.
Remember how you
responded to scolding when
you were a young child.*

Read in a very critical voice . . .
  *"You are uncooperative. You
  come late, and you think it
  doesn't make any difference.
  Hurry up. You didn't do it
  well enough. How come you
  don't do better? I want you to
  hurry! You are not paying
  attention! I have told you a
  hundred times how to do
  that. Now shape up!"*

Say: *Will you come back to the
present and give up any
negative feelings?*

Ask: *Will you take me out of the
role play and see me as I
am?*

Ask: *Will you report what you wanted to do with your balloons and what your feelings were?*
EXAMPLES:
sad, mad, irritated, scared, "What did I do wrong?" "I didn't do it," tuned it out, wanted to hit, broke the balloon.

Ask: *Will someone who knows about the Spontaneous and Adaptive Part describe it?*

If the following ideas were not covered in the description, point to the **four part** list as you talk.

Say: *Those of us who had fun and laughed were experiencing the spontaneous aspect of the Spontaneous and Adaptive Part. Those of us who played out the feelings from the scolding may have felt sad, scared, or rebellious in the way that we did when we were young. We were experiencing the Adaptive Part. When we were being scolded, some of us may have chosen to get into the Problem Solving Part of our personalities and to watch and listen but not to pick up on the scolded feelings.*

Hand out the **Four Responses from the Spontaneous and Adaptive Part** sheet, Meeting 5, page 156.

Say: *We have a Spontaneous and Adaptive Part in us all our lives. We initiate many things from our Spontaneous and Adaptive Part—good times, inventions, dreams. We also can do a lot of responding from our Spontaneous and Adaptive Part. This role play will show four different ways a person can respond from the Spontaneous and Adaptive Part.*

Ask: *Will five people do a role play with me? After I describe each role, I will read a statement to you. One of you will respond in a **Free** way, one in a **Compliant** way, one in a **Rebellious** way, one in an **Ingenious** way.*

Hand out the four signs reading "**Free**," "**Compliant**," "**Rebellious**," and "**Ingenious**." Indicate who will play Aunt Mable.
Stand before the person with the sign as you tell about each role.

Say: *Here are your instructions: Spontaneous or **Free part,** you like to move about, play ball, dance, do big muscle activities. When you are positive you give love, verve, and excitement to life. You are negative if you are allowed to take over at inappropriate times. This does not apply to babies who use their Free part to let adults know when they need care.*
*   **Compliant** part, you reflect some of the ways in which caring for oneself and living with other people impose upon your freedom.*

147

"Housekeeping" is necessary but may not be enjoyable. You are positive when your compliance helps you get along in life and negative when you sit back and let other people make your decisions.

Rebellious part, you are positive when your stubbornness helps you survive. You are negative when you say: "I hate to follow directions or be on time," or "Nobody can tell me what speed to drive at as long as there's not a cop around." You and the Compliant part are the flip side of each other. If Mother says, "Wear your rubbers when it rains," and compliant always wears rubbers when it rains, Mother is in charge. If you never wear rubbers when it rains because you are rebelling against Mother, she is still in charge. Both of you, compliant and rebellious, engage in adaptive behavior. You let Mother think for you. Some people do this all their lives, even after Mother is dead. If I do this I am letting the mother in my head run my life with rules that made sense to her when I was a little girl. I can choose to use my Problem Solving Part to update those rules and run my own life.

Ingenious, or tricky little professor, you figure things out; you find ways to say yes and mean no. You are intuitive and creative. You are positive when you "psyche out" life to help solve problems and negative when your trickiness gets you into trouble. A person who is often evasive or manipulative should consider spending more time in the Problem Solving Part and less time in the Ingenious part.

Say: Get into the posture and tone of voice expressive of the role. Feel free to elaborate. Get help from the other participants if you want to. Aunt Mable, please think of how the different responses feel to you.

Read the six directives that begin "Hug your Aunt Mable" on page 158.

Let each of the four people respond to each directive.

Ask: Aunt Mable, will you tell us how you felt about each of these four?

Say: Each of the four Spontaneous and Adaptive Parts can be a positive or negative response.

Ask: Will someone point out a negative example of each of the four?

Say: It is important to encourage and nourish the positive parts of the Spontaneous and Adaptive Part.

Hand out **How to Strengthen the Spontaneous and Adaptive Part** sheet and ask people to take it home and do several items from it.

Say: *One way to strengthen the Spontaneous and Adaptive Part is to praise appropriate spontaneous and adaptive behavior. Use page 75 in the text to plan strokes for the Nurturing and Structuring Part, the Problem Solving Part, and the Spontaneous and Adaptive Part of someone. This encourages three strong parts of one's personality.*

Ask: *How many people wrote examples on page 107? Remember—writing helps many of us turn our wishes into behavior.*

5. FOUR WAYS OF PARENTING *(10 Minutes)*

Say: *Another way to strengthen the Spontaneous and Adaptive Part is to provide strong nurturing and structuring to protect it.*

If the group did not do a Four Ways of Parenting at goal setting time, do one now.

Ask: *Will five of you do the Four Parent on page 72 of your text? Will the rest of you listen carefully to which message would encourage, in either a negative or a positive way, the free child? Which would encourage the adaptive, which the rebellious, and which the ingenious?*

Ask: *Has anyone heard examples of discounting during the Four Parent exercise?*

If so, identify what was discounted—self, situation, or others.

OPTIONAL:
Ask: Will you identify which of the following statements discounts self, others, or situation?
- No point in asking Mom. She's grumpy today. I know she won't let us go. (other)
- I could never learn to do ceramics. (self)
- I don't carry liability insurance because a disaster couldn't happen to me. (situation)

---

6. SEPARATING SEX AND NURTURING[2]
(5 Minutes)

Say: *Another way to care for the Spontaneous and Adaptive Part is to differentiate between sexual strokes and nurturing.*

Say: *People have varying needs for nurturing all their lives. Sometimes they don't get the nurturing they need or want as adults because they have the idea that adult touching can only be sexual.*
EXAMPLES:
"Men and women who touch each other must have

149

something going." or "People of the same sex who touch each other look 'queer'." Some men feel free to touch each other only on the playing field, where it is OK for men to bash each other with their bodies during a football play or to hug each other after a touchdown.

Say: *Sexual touching is only one kind of pleasurable touching. Many people also like to be touched in a nurturing, supportive way. For example: Fred, age forty-five, said after the funeral of his nephew, "I hugged my brother. It felt so good! I haven't touched him since we were boys. I wish I could hug him each time I see him. I'm very fond of him, but I guess I don't show it much."*

Jessica, the mother of six-week-old Tim, said, "Sometimes I get so tired by the time my husband, Jim, gets home, I just want him to take care of me." And Jim says, "Sometimes Jessica seems to have forgotten about me—it's the baby this and the baby that, and I know she is busy, but sometimes I wish she would find a little time to take care of me the way she used to."

Ask: *Will those of you who want to participate in the exercise make a Separating Sex and Nurturing pact with someone? It could sound something like this: "For*

twenty minutes I will give you nurturing without sexual approaches. I will listen to you, or hug you, or whatever you want." The other person responds, "All right, today I want you to make me cocoa and cinnamon toast and pay attention just to me for the whole twenty minutes and not answer the telephone or the door bell. Next time I may want you to hold me, but today it's cocoa and cinnamon toast."

If you do most of your sexual touching in the bedroom, start your nurturing pacts someplace else to help you separate nurturing touch and sexual touch.

Ask: *Will you carry out your agreement before the next meeting and then think about how you like it?*

Say: *Nurturing is a function of the Nurturing and Structuring Part. If you have a Separating Sex and Nurturing pact with someone, you are strengthening your own Nurturing and Structuring Part when you find out how they want to be nurtured and do what they want. You also strengthen your Nurturing and Structuring Part and improve your ability to take care of yourself when you ask them to nurture you in the exact way that you want to be nurtured. You strengthen your Spontaneous and*

Adaptive Part when you accept the nurturing and when you enjoy sex.

Hand out **Time Out for Nurturing** on page *161* for a take-home activity.

Say: *This activity, Time Out for Nurturing, can be used to strengthen the quality of nurturing in a whole family. If you think you may have difficulty with a Separating Sex and Nurturing pact, try the whole family nurturing activity described in Time Out for Nurturing first.*

7. AFFIRMATIONS FOR DOING *(10 Minutes)*

Ask: *Does anyone want to share a*
✱ *way in which you affirmed thinking, page 112 in text?*

Point to the **Affirmations for Doing** poster.

Say: *The Affirmations for Doing are important for high self-esteem in six- to eighteen-month-old children, thirteen and fourteen year olds, people who are starting a new job, a new relationship, learning any new skill, and for everyone else.*

Read the **Affirmations for Doing** poster.

AFFIRMATIONS FOR DOING
You can get attention or approval and still act the way you really feel.

You can do things and get support at the same time.

It's OK to explore and experiment.

It's OK for you to initiate.

You can be curious and intuitive.

Say: *I invite you to go on a Doing New Things Fantasy Trip. These Doing affirmations help to free people to explore and learn new skills. They help separate acceptance of the person from her behavior. This is a fantasy trip to a place where you can do something you have always wanted to do. I am here and I will protect you. You can come back at any time during the trip, or I will bring you back at the end. Get in a comfortable position. Close your eyes and breathe deeply. Hear the sounds in this room. Let them go. Smell the odors in this room. Let them go. Feel the air entering and leaving your body; feel the weight of your body against the floor or the chair. Let those feelings go.*
Imagine that you are in a room supplied with all the

materials and equipment needed for you to do something you have always wanted to try doing. It may be an artist's studio, a machine shop, a computer room with lots of peripheral equipment, a fabulously equipped gym, a stage, a decorator's shop with stunning samples—whatever.

As you walk in and decide what you will try first, listen to these messages: "I see you are starting to do these things on your own. That may be exciting or it may be scary, but, remember, no matter how well you do or even if you don't do anything at all, I love you. It is all right for you to go ahead and try things. I see that you are curious; that's wonderful. You can initiate things and figure things out and be intuitive. I am here, and I will watch over you, encourage you, and protect you. I will not let you hurt yourself or anyone else or this wonderful room. Go ahead and explore."

After three or four minutes . . .

Say: *Finish your fantasy and come back to this room. Be in the present. See, hear, smell, and feel here, now. Think about which message or messages were most helpful to you.*

Ask: *For how many of you did the messages help you to*

separate doing from being accepted as a person?

Say: *Turn to the Affirmations for Doing in the text, page 83.*

Ask: *Will you write on page 83 the affirmations you liked hearing in the fantasy?*

Ask: *Do you prefer those messages the way they are written on the poster or the way they are written on page 83 in the text?*

Say: *When you plan your messages for a toddler, remember that toddlers learn from the way they are touched and from your tone of voice. Although they may not understand words, they can sense the meaning.*

Say: *You can give these affirmations to yourselves. You can think of things you especially need to hear. Don wrote "I am an all-right person and I can find safe places and ways to try new things." He taped it up in the bathroom where he could read it every morning while he brushed his teeth. Jane wrote "I can be important without being cute." She put it in her top desk drawer.*

Say: *On page 83 write affirmations for someone else and for yourself, and practice before the next meeting getting and giving those messages you believe.*

152

8. RESPONSIBILITY
(15 Minutes)

Say: *At the last meeting we did the Eat Your Beans for Mommy exercise. Since our last meeting, did any of you recognize a statement adults use that invites children to take care of the adults' feelings?*

Say: *"You can get attention or approval and still act the way you feel" means that adults refrain from thinking and feeling for children. This is the fourth exercise on encouraging responsibility. It is called You Are Going to Love This.*

Say: *One of the ways adults can forget to invite children to take responsibility for their own feelings and thinking is to speak and act as if they are thinking and feeling for the children. We will take some common expressions that suggest how people should feel and think and change them into sentences that invite people to be responsible for their own thinking and feeling.*

Ask: *Will you work in pairs?*

Hand to each person a card on which is written one of the following:

1. I have something to tell you that you aren't going to like.

2. You will think this is a great idea!
3. I know that you feel bad because you hurt my feelings.
4. I have two pieces of bad news and one of good news.
5. That makes you so scared you can't think, doesn't it?
6. You are going to love this!
7. The message you gave her made her feel like she couldn't succeed.
8. Scared? You don't have anything to be scared about!
9. This book will help you, but you will just hate it.
10. I see that you are depressed. Cheer up.
11. This story will make you laugh!
12. You won't tell me what you need, so I'll go ahead and take care of you.
13. If I ask, you won't tell the truth, so I won't ask. I'll decide what you want me to do.

Give the following directions all at once:

Say: *One of you read the message that is on the card. Other person, do not respond to the message, but think of how you feel. Become aware of how the message invites you to let someone else think or feel for you. Tell your partner how you feel.*

After about two minutes . . .
Call the attention of the group and

153

Ask: *Will each of you who received a message tell how you felt?*

Say: *Rewrite the message on the opposite side of the card in a way that invites the other person to be responsible for her feelings and thoughts.*
EXAMPLE:
That arm really hurts, doesn't it? Changed to: Does your arm hurt?
After about three minutes . . .

Ask: *Will each pair read the first statement and the rewritten statement for the whole group?*

OPTIONAL:
For each developmental stage indicate two ways in which one could tell a child it is time for a bath: a way that invites dependency and a way that invites responsibility.

Say: *It is especially important not to think and feel for children from six to eighteen months. They are learning to trust their own senses to provide them with data for thinking. It is also important not to think and feel for children eighteen months to three years old who are deciding to trust their own ability to think. It is important not to think and feel for people of all ages who want to be responsible, independent thinkers.*

Ask: *Between now and the next meeting, will you practice inviting people to think and feel for themselves?*

OPTIONAL:
9. PARENTING TIPS
(5-10 Minutes)

Ask: *Does anyone have any thoughts or questions to*
✳ *share about the Parenting Tips on pages 70 and 71 or about Chapter three?*

Say: *The tips for parenting six- to eighteen-month-old toddlers suggest that parents of toddlers need lots of strokes. A Separating Sex and Nurturing pact can be used by parents to get more strokes of both kinds.*

If there is anyone in the group with a toddler, do a Suggestion Circle on ways in which parents of toddlers can get nurturing from people other than their spouses.

Ask: *Does anyone want to report any thoughts since our last*
✳ *meeting about the ways of handling angry-acting two year olds?*

---

10. ADDITIONS

Address any items added during goal setting.

CLOSING

Take care of any business details. Point to the **Goals** poster and briefly note the content covered. Review the homework for the next meeting:

1. *Practice Rejecting Destructive Strokes while standing centered in front of a mirror.*
2. *Make a Separating Sex and Nurturing pact if you want to.*
3. *Stroke all three Parts of the Personality for someone, page 75 in text.*
4. *Strengthen your Spontaneous and Adaptive Part by playing for ten hours during the coming week.*
5. *Practice the Affirmations for Doing on somebody.*
6. *Practice encouraging people to be responsible for their own feelings and thinking.*
7. *Read Chapter five and page 260.*

Say: *You can start on your ten hours of playing by joining me in a quick round of "London Bridge Is Falling Down."*

Play London Bridge.

Ask: *Any Resentments and Appreciations?*

Say: *Thank you. The meeting is closed. I will see you at the next meeting.*

Spontaneous and Adaptive Part of the Personality

1. The Spontaneous Part of us is present from birth.
2. It has lots of feelings.
3. It needs to be cared for by nurturing people. When we become adults the Spontaneous and Adaptive Part of us needs to be nurtured by the Nurturing and Structuring Part of us, by others, and by society.
4. A person whose Spontaneous and Adaptive Part is functioning well and is well cared for is attractive, creative, intuitive, exciting, and fun to be with.
5. The Spontaneous Part of us responds freely to our external and internal environments and can have positive or negative feelings.

SPONTANEOUS OR FREE	*Positive*	*Negative*
	fun, curious, sensuous, sexy, joyful, indignant, spontaneous, affectionate, energetic	angry, despairing, fearful

The Adaptive Part of us can be compliant or rebellious or ingenious. Each of these responses can be either positive or negative.

COMPLIANT	*Positive*	*Negative*
	mannerly, housebroken, scared, able to move through guilt to resolution	scared, wallowing in guilt, avoiding //resolution

REBELLIOUS

Positive
determined, stubborn
(tenacious), resistant to
dictators

Negative
insubordinate,
stubborn (rigid),
vengeful

INGENIOUS

Positive
inventive, clever,
amusing, hunch-playing,
manipulative
(to survive)

Negative
slippery, devious,
manipulative
(to put others down)

Responses from the Spontaneous and Adaptive Part

Directives
1. Hug your Aunt Mable.
2. Don't track mud in the house.
3. Do a good job on that.
4. You are invited to a "dress up" party.
5. That was a stupid thing to do, dummy!
6. Drink this poison.

Free Part (Spontaneous) Response
"Here's what I want to do!" (spontaneous, capable of great joy, great rage, this quality is present at birth)

1. Impulsively hugs or spontaneously draws back.
2. Tracks. (without thinking, is amazed that mud could be so important when the ice cream truck is coming)
3. "A good job? Who, me? You think I can do that? Wow!" (excited, or happy or scared or all three)
4. "A party? Wow, let's go! I want to wear the outfit I feel great in!"
5. "Dumb? Ouch, that hurts. I feel mad, too!"
6. Runs away.

Rebellious Part (Adaptive) Response
"If you want me to do it, I won't!" (learned coping skill, rebellious)

1. Doesn't hug.
2. Tracks. (defiantly)
3. "So you want me to do a good job? Ha, ha, watch me fail."
4. "I heard this is a formal party, so I'll wear old clothes to show them I don't have to conform."
5. You told me I'm dumb—I'll show you—I'll be the smartest person you ever saw!"
6. "No way."

Compliant Part (Adaptive) Response

"If you want me to do it, I'll do it." (learned coping skill, pleasing)

1. Hugs obediently.
2. Doesn't track.
3. "You want me to do a good job? All right. I'll try till I get it perfect."
4. "I certainly hope I'm wearing the proper clothes for this party."
5. "You told me I'm dumb, so I must be dumb."
6. Drinks the poison.

Ingenious Part (Adaptive) Response

"If you want me to do it, maybe, I'll see." (learned coping skill, tricky)

1. "I'll hug her after this TV show is over."
2. "Tracks. Must have been the dog."
3. "You want me to do a good job on that. I'd be glad to after I get the tools (time, energy, help, skill, etc.)."
4. "Formal, huh? I don't feel like wearing formal clothes, so I'll wear my grubbies and tell the hostess my good clothes got lost at the cleaners."
5. "You told me I'm dumb, OK. I'll remember that and use it later to trick Mom."
6. "Let me take it to the next room and drink it." (pours the poison out)

How to Strengthen Your Spontaneous and Adaptive Part

1. Dance, sing, skip, hop, slide, skate, build sand castles.
2. Practice being considerate, use good manners.
3. Compromise.
4. Let someone take care of you.
5. Practice feeling an appropriate amount of guilt if you have hurt someone. Do something to make amends to that person.
6. Make a fun list and do some of the things on it.
7. Separate Sex and Nurturing.
8. Take time out for nurturing.

Time Out for Nurturing

Here is a way to carve some time from the usual press of daily activities to receive concentrated nurturing. It strengthens the Spontaneous and Adaptive Part of the person being nurtured. It usually will increase spontaneity, creativity, and a sense of well-being. It also strengthens the Nurturing and Structuring Part of the people who are doing the nurturing. It encourages young children to develop nurturing skills and gives them a chance to practice taking care of big people in a positive "nurturing" way. This is in contrast to the negative "being responsible for or taking care of big people" that is referred to in the Affirmations for Thinking and in Eat Your Beans for Mommy.

Two or more people make a Time Out for Nurturing contract.

1. They draw straws to see who gets the first time out.
2. Evie draws the winning straw. She decides what kind of nurturing she wants and for how long. If Evie has strong rules about deserving or earning strokes, she should make the time short enough so that she does not feel uncomfortable. Any amount of time is OK. Four hours? Half an hour? Five minutes? However long Evie wants is the right amount of time. She chooses an afternoon at the zoo, a leisurely dinner cooked and served by someone else, an afternoon of sports, a ten-minute back rub, whatever the little girl inside Evie wants.
3. Evie negotiates with the nurturers to see if they are willing and able to give her what she wants and changes her plan if necessary. If there are children involved, Evie will have to adapt to their abilities.
4. The nurturers make all the arrangements and carry out the time for nurturing by providing structure, protection, and strokes.
5. Evie accepts the nurturing, lets the good feelings in, and refrains from taking care of other people during the time out.
6. The group sets a time for the next person's Time Out for Nurturing.

Homework

1. Practice Rejecting Toxic Strokes centered and uncentered.
2. Make a Separating Sex and Nurturing pact.
3. Stroke all three Parts of the Personality of someone.
4. Strengthen your Spontaneous and Adaptive Part by playing ten hours this week.
5. Practice Affirmations for Doing, page 83.
6. Practice thinking and feeling for self.
7. Read Chapter five and page 260.

Notes

1. Clyde Reid, *Celebrate the Temporary* (New York: Harper and Row, 1972).
2. Thanks for the idea of Separating Sex and Nurturing to Terri and Jerry White of Peninsula Institute, Palo Alto, California.

LETTER TO MARJ 6

Dear Marj,

Meeting six. Ah, yes. Tell me, Marj, do you ever notice those numbers that suggest time for each section and think that the time is short? I do. And I used to worry about it, but I don't anymore. Not since I watched Sheila Hartmann do Meeting 6. I now believe that almost anything is possible! Before the meeting started, three people told Sheila they wanted the group to do Four Ways of Parenting exercises for them. She said, "OK, right after we review the goals." She moved through the **Name Tag** exercise, the **Ground Rules,** and the **Goals.** As she handed out the Four Ways of Parenting signs she reminded the group that they were especially good at doing that exercise. They worked quickly; they switched roles; they offered suggestions for alternative ways to play each role.

When the first three people had finished hearing their four messages, more people asked to sit on the chair. Stress must have been marching through their neighborhood that week. Sheila flowed with the group. An hour and twenty minutes into the session someone said, "I have a problem I want to hear the Four Parent messages for, but I know you have new ideas for us, Sheila, so I'll wait and see if anyone will stay after class and role play with me." My mind raced through the material. What would I skip if I were the leader? Only forty minutes left. Obviously Sheila had been doing what the group needed, but what would she do with the two hours of material? She asked the group what they wanted. They said, "If you will move right through it, we'll get as much out of it as we can." She talked fast, they jumped into the role plays, and she covered it all! No problem. They raced along beside her with apparent ease. I grant you, there wasn't much discussion, but they seemed to grasp the concepts, and the following week they didn't show any lack of understanding. Incredible!

It seemed as if the people, having had their own needs met, had increased energy and clear thinking channels with which to grasp new material. This was a good lesson for me: "Don't assume that I have to skip content because the time is short!"

So here it is:

The **Names** exercise encourages the Spontaneous and Adaptive part to grow.

Are people asking for strokes? Are you? It may be uncomfortable at first, but it is so important! During the winter in which my father-in-law was dying of cancer, my nephew was in a terrifying auto accident, and my friend Sally's daughter was in a coma, I would go to class with a pale face and low energy level. When I explained that I needed strokes and energy, people were willing to help me. It took about one minute for them to give me sympathy and encouragement. It did not drain energy from them. We all functioned better, and I left with more energy than I had when I arrived. Don't wait for disaster! Ask whenever you want strokes.

The **Ground Rules** are still important! They give protection.

Be sure to post the **Goals** where everyone can see them. That helps the people who like visual reinforcement and the people who like to know the sequence of learnings.

1. I do not encourage talking while people are walking around the **Stroke Buffet.** It was designed to help people think about their own or someone else's messages. If someone does talk about negative messages, be sure to point out that she had some positives and to count them also. This exercise often helps foster parents get insights into why a particular child has chosen to use some behavior that is dysfunctional in his current setting.

   I also admire this exercise and the way people use it for themselves. I write messages from the text, pages 235 and 236, on many colors of paper. The other day on my way to a meeting, I picked up my pack of messages and glanced through them. Most of them were not in my handwriting, and they were not the messages on the list. Apparently people had picked up my messages and had torn them up or kept them and I had collected other people's messages. Lots of my favorite messages were missing! I did not have time to make new cards—I had to use what was there and see what would happen. There was no problem. People got the idea. They picked out messages and wrote their own. Relax, Jean, and believe in the power of the learner.

2. **Affirmations for Identity and Power** are zingy affirmations! Power is neat stuff! Power is the ability to keep the things we want to keep and to change the things we want to change. It is the ability to stay alive![1] If you encounter someone who believes he has to choose between being powerful and having needs, invite him to consider how he limits himself whenever he is thinking from an either/or position. He can ask himself, "What are three ways of handling this situation?" He can list and resist sayings that encourage him to stay in an either/or position. Example: "One of two things will happen, either you will like it or you won't."

   People will probably be reporting some creative and exciting ways of giving affirmations by now. Annette Pattie writes them on separate cards with little pictures, puts them in a jar, and encourages her children to bring her one when they want to hear it. Four-year-old Christopher knows which picture goes with which messages, and when he brings Annette a card, she gives him a snuggle with the message and lots of approval for knowing what he needs and getting what he wants.

3. **Rejecting Toxic Strokes from All Three Parts of the Personality** is for some persons the most powerful exercise in all the meetings. The ten minutes spent reviewing all three parts of the personality help people get ready for the exercise.

    Make the distinction between negatives that are destructive ("You are an awful person"), which should be thrown away for the person's health, and negatives that ask the person to improve his performance ("There are too many typing errors in this letter; you can do better"), which is helpful to the person.

    Write each set of messages, pages 182-183, on one card. If you don't feel confident enough to lead this exercise, walk and talk your way through each set ahead of time, or get some friends to do the role plays so you can observe and think about them. I was watching Marianne Erlien facilitate this exercise when the person who was rejecting "You are a bad person!" had difficulty throwing it away. Almost instantly, Marianne had another person on his feet demonstrating how to reject that stroke from the same part of the personality. It was a powerful display of options. Marianne had refrained from moralizing, and I admired that.

4. I'll Do It Later and other ways of Saying No Crooked is the **Responsibility** exercise that focuses on getting straight yes or no responses to requests. This is another exercise that often brings groans. But people do jump into it and seem to appreciate yet another way to improve their communication skills.

5. Keep **Four Ways of Parenting** in the present. If someone wants to go back to a problem he had as a youngster, have him stay in his present age and ask what an adult who had this problem years ago should do now.

    Remember that the Four Ways of Parenting exercise is done from the Nurturing and Structuring part, so it contains how to's, beliefs, values and prejudices. It offers love, advice and opinions. There are *many* ways to play *each* of the four roles reflecting differences in people's value systems.

6. **Tips for Parenting** the child from three to six years is an optional exercise. Encourage parents to take care of themselves. Constant questions are so important yet so tiring! Offer encouragement to people to parent well even though they are sometimes tired, perplexed, or overwhelmed.

I hope you are giving time for Resentments and Appreciations during the **closing.** Have a terrific meeting!
Love,

Jean

P.S. Let me know when you will be in town so we can talk and party!

MEETING 6

BEFORE MEETING 6

1. Study Meeting 6 plan.
2. Reread Chapter five and study Stroke Buffet, pages 257, 258, 222-225 and 235, 236 and 262, 265 and 274 in text.
3. Read the sixth Letter to Marj.
4. Reread "Who, Me, Lead a Group?", Question 7.
5. Collect the following **supplies** :
   paper for name tags
   felt tip pens
   tape
   balloons
   3x5 cards—three per participant
   seven squares of paper per participant
6. Make or collect the following **visual aids**:

POSTERS
- Ground Rules, Meeting 1, page 37
- Meeting 6 Goals, Meeting 6, page 170
- All six Affirmation posters, Meeting 2, page 63

CARDS AND SIGNS
- Stroke Buffet Messages, *Self-Esteem: A Family Affair*, pages 235 and 236.
- Three Parts of Personality circles
- Three Parts of Personality Review cards, Meeting 6, page 174
- Five sets of cards for Rejecting Toxic Strokes. Make two copies of each card, one for the sender and one for the rejector. Meeting 6, pages 182-183
- Cards for I'll Do It Later exercise, Meeting 6, pages 177-178
- Affirmation cymbals for Power and Identity, Marj 2, page 58.
  DUPLICATED HANDOUT
- Homework, Meeting 6, page 184

OPENING *(10 Minutes)*
Post the posters.

NAMES
Hand out name tags and pens.

Ask: *Will you find someone you have not worked with before, write his name on the name tag, find out where his Stroke Bank level is, and find out three ways he plans to have fun during the coming year? Write words or draw pictures on his name tag to tell how he will have fun.*

Ask: *Will you introduce your partner, indicate his Stroke Bank level, and tell one or more ways he plans to have fun?*

Say: *Some people raise their Stroke Bank levels by having fun or thinking about having fun. This also strengthens the Spontaneous and Adaptive Part of the personality.*

Ask: *Have any of you raised your Stroke Level since you came into the room? If any of you want to raise your Stroke Level by asking for strokes,* *will you do that now? Will someone report on how you spread ten hours of play throughout the week and what was the most fun?*

GROUND RULES

Point to the **Ground Rules** poster. Read the Ground Rules.

Ask: *Which Ground Rule is the most helpful in creating an atmosphere of respect?*

GOALS

Post the **Meeting 6** goals.

MEETING 6 GOALS
1. Stroke Buffet
2. Affirmations for Identity and Power
3. Rejecting Toxic Strokes
4. Responsibility
5. Four Ways of Parenting
6. Parenting Tips
7. Additions
8. Celebrations

Read and negotiate the goals.
1. **Stroke Buffet** —*We will choose messages from the Stroke Buffet and consider what to do about them.*
2. **Affirmations for Identity and Power** —*We will practice them.*

3. **Rejecting Toxic Strokes from all three Parts of the Personality** —*We will practice them also.*
4. **Responsibility** —*We will encourage responsibility by recognizing ways of saying no crooked and by practicing ways of inviting children to say no responsibly.*
5. **Four Ways of Parenting** —*We will practice them.*
6. **Parenting Tips** —*Does anyone want time to discuss Parenting Tips for three- to six-year-old children?*
7. **Additions** —*Does anyone have suggestions for topics to be addressed by a Suggestion Circle or a Four Parent?*
8. *Does anyone want to share a* **Celebration?** (Do so now.)

1. STROKE BUFFET[2]
(15-20 Minutes)

Place the **Stroke Buffet** messages (pages 235-236 in text, Early Messages I Chose to Hear) on the floor and spread them so that people can walk among them. Or place them on a large table so people can walk around the table and look at them.
Give each person six or seven squares of blank paper.

Say: *The Stroke Buffet exercise allows us to think about some of the messages we have heard and some of the messages we have chosen to believe or to reject. It expands on the Stroke Quotient Decision Theory* that we explored at the last meeting. Does anyone want to share any further thoughts, feelings, or opinions about the Stroke Quotient Decision Theory?

Hold up the text open to page 81.

Say: *One part of the Stroke Quotient Decision Theory is the idea that people believed messages that helped them choose their Stroke Quotients. In order to explore this theory, we will look at a variety of messages, pick up some, and later consider what we want to do with them.*

Ask: *Will you walk around and read the messages and consider which of those messages were offered to you when you were little?*

OPTIONAL:
Person may select a specific child and guess which messages that child has "picked up" so far.

Ask: *Will you pick up or copy the messages that were very loud or important to you?*

Ask: *Will you write any additional loud messages that you heard that are not among the ones displayed?*

Say: *Keep them to yourself. Do not show them to anybody.*

After five minutes reassemble people.

Ask: *How many of you saw messages that were offered to you as a child but which you did not pick up and make important for yourself?*

Say: *Think about the stroke quotient you identified for yourself at the last meeting. Do any of the messages that you have in your hand help to explain how you chose that particular stroke quotient? If your stroke quotient is higher than the messages would suggest, have you revised some old messages or chosen new ones?*

Ask: *If you have a negative message, will you write a new one to replace it? You may want to think about the affirmations we have studied to help you choose new ones.*

Allow two or three minutes for writing.

Ask: *Will you consider each message in your hand and think of ways you have used it to get along or to survive? Some people had more positive messages from which to choose than other people had, but since we choose to keep our messages we can also choose to replace the negative with positive ones. If you have chosen a new message and are ready to tear up an old one, you may do that now.*

Say: *Our children choose the messages that they pick up.*

Adults are responsible for the quality of messages they offer. One way to invite positive self-esteem in children is to improve the quality of the Being, Doing well, and Can-do-better messages that we place on our child's stroke buffet table and to refrain from offering Plastic messages or Don't be messages.

2. AFFIRMATIONS FOR IDENTITY AND POWER *(15 Minutes)*

Ask: *Does anyone want to tell us how you got some Affirmations for Doing?*

✳

Ask: *What new ways have you invented to give the Affirmations?*

Say: *Affirmations for Identity and Power, for learning who we are, are important for children three to six years old, for middle teenagers, (15-17), for people who own their power to be who they are, who ask straight for what they need. They are helpful for people who are giving up inadequate ways of dealing with life and incorporating healthier ways, and for everyone else.*

Point to and read the **Affirmations for Identity and Power** poster:

AFFIRMATIONS FOR
IDENTITY AND POWER

You can be powerful
and still have needs.
You don't have to act
scary, sick, sad, or mad
to get taken care of.
It's OK for you to
explore who you are.
It's important for you to
find out what you're
about.
It's OK to imagine
things without being
afraid you'll make
them come true.
It's OK to find out the
consequences of your
own behavior.

Say: *These messages help the child who is three, four or five years old discover who he is. The child will be continuing to learn about cause-and-effect and should start to differentiate between feelings and actions and to ask straight for what he needs. These messages are also especially important for fifteen- to eighteen-year-old people as they recycle old behaviors and attempt to resolve earlier problems. These messages are helpful to anyone who is learning to be more direct and less manipulative.*

Hand out four 3x5 cards to each person.

Say: *This exercise allows us to explore which of these affirmations is helpful for us today.*

Ask: *Will you write the affirmations using your own names?*

Read:
> "I, _____,
> can be powerful and still have needs."
> "I, _____,
> don't have to act scary, sick, sad, mad, happy, cute, or strong to get taken care of."
> "I, _____,
> can express my feelings straight without inviting other people to be responsible for my feelings."

Ask: *Will you read the messages aloud in unison?*

Ask: *Which one sounded especially helpful to you?*

Say: *If any of you read a message that you believe is not true in your life (but I do have to act mad before people will pay attention to me), you can think about whether you want to continue that way or if you want to change it.*

Say: *Sometimes people change the messages as they write. That can be a clue to what they need to hear. Lorrie Casselton, who has altered her alcoholism identity, wrote "I, Lorrie, can be powerful and still have me." Then she said, "Wow, I can't stay alive without power! I have been afraid that if I acted powerful I wouldn't*

stay alive. I'm going to work that out because everyone needs to be powerful and that includes me!"*

Ask: *Will you write on page 143 in the text three ways in which you can give these Affirmations for Identity and Power to yourself and others? Add the "imagine" affirmation if you want to. Please answer these questions internally: Will you plan to get the messages from more than one source? Will you teach your children to find lots of sources? Will you practice getting and giving those messages before the next meeting?*

3. REJECTING TOXIC STROKES[3]
(30 Minutes)

Place three large circles marked **"Nurturing and Structuring," "Problem Solving,"** and **"Spontaneous and Adaptive"** on the floor to represent the Three Parts of the Personality.

Say: *Before we practice Rejecting Toxic Strokes from all Three Parts of the Personality, let us do a quick review of all three.[4]*

Shuffle cards which have on one side a word or words significant to Personality Part and on the reverse side the initials of that Part of the Personality. Hand a few to each participant.

Review of Parts of the Personality

Write or print each of the following words or phases on a card. On the back of the card write the initials of the part of the personality that word or phrase suggests.

N.S. on the back	P.S. on the back	S.A. on the back
approve, disapprove	one, two, three, four, five, six, etc.	entertainers, inventors, clowns,
vice, sin	what if . . . ?	yuk!
should, ought	puzzle	slippery, devious
right, wrong	when, where, how?	whatever you say
rules	estimate	wow!
protection	find out	stubborn, tenacious
culture	engineer, computer programmer, accountant	I don't wanna
teachers, ministers, social workers	$12 \times 9 = ?$	fun, rage, despair
bad, good	I think . . .	sob
nurturing	problem-solving	magic, sexy, greedy, vain, spiteful
automatic skills	frequently	"Yes, sir, right now!"
I believe	often	I want, I wish, I'll try

Say: *Will each of you read your cards and place them on the circle that each is associated with? Will the rest of you watch to see if the card is correctly placed? (You can check on the back of the card.)*

Leave the circles and cards on the floor for reference during the Rejecting Toxic Strokes exercise.

✳ Ask: *Does anyone want to tell us how you practiced stroking the Problem Solving Part and Spontaneous and Adaptive Part? (Use page 75 in the text.) Now will you use page 141 to plan ways to stroke all three Parts of the Personality of someone before our next meeting?*

Say: *Destructive or **toxic strokes** are just that—poison. They do not help us grow. Negative strokes that help us grow are not poison, although we may not like hearing them. At our last meeting we practiced rejecting destructive strokes by Centering. Now we have experienced all three parts of the personality, and we will demonstrate rejecting strokes from each. People can choose the Part of the Personality from which to initiate and to respond to communications. Part of positive self-esteem is the ability to identify and throw away negations or destructive strokes such as Plastics or Don't be messages. We can offer children this positive self-esteem-building skill by modeling for them how to reject toxic strokes from each Part of our Personality. We show them how we reject* destructive strokes by nurturing or setting limits from our Nurturing and Structuring Part, by thinking from our Problem Solving Part, or by a childlike response from our Spontaneous and Adaptive Part.

Say: *This is a role play that allows someone to practice choosing the Part of the Personality from which to reject destructive strokes. There are cards for you to read and you may add examples of your own. Watch for actions and listen for words. The toxic strokes are:*
Set 1: You are a bad person.
Set 2: You stink.
Set 3: Why did you do that terrible thing?
Set 4: You want help with your problem? Your problems are not important!
Set 5: Why have you suddenly changed the way you discipline the kids?
Set 6: Oh! You don't work, you just take care of kids (or baby-sit).

Ask the person reading the toxic strokes:
Will you stand to one side wearing the Criticizing sign from the Four Parent exercise and deliver the destructive messages three or four times, with feeling, allowing time in between for the stroke to be rejected?

Ask the rejecting person:
Will you stand on the

designated marker as you read the rejection? Use appropriate voice inflection and body posture for each Part of the Personality.

Ask: *Will the group observe whether the person seems to be throwing away the bad stroke, keeping it, or attacking or "getting" the sender?*

Ask the person who will reject:
Which stroke do you want to practice rejecting?

Hand each person the appropriate set of cards.
Have the sender say the toxic strokes and the rejector read the responses on the cards.

Ask the Rejector after each role play:
Was it easier for you to throw away or reject the toxic strokes from one part of the personality?
Was there one in which you rejected the stroke and did not put the other person down?
Was there one in which you "got" the sender?

Say: *There are no correct answers. How to throw away toxic strokes is an individual decision.*

Ask: *Does anyone who was observing want to share an observation?*

Use more sets if you have time.

Say: *We are responsible for letting strokes in or keeping them out. We will practice more*

175

sets or you may choose toxic strokes to reject at Meetings 7 and 8.

OPTIONAL:
Ask if someone wants to choose a destructive criticism that he finds hard to reject but really should. If so, have him tell the criticism to the sender. The rejector will throw away the criticism from each part of his personality, remembering that he can ask for help from the group.

Debrief the role players.

Ask: *Will you keep the skill you have practiced and let go any negative feelings you may have had during the role play? Will you see the people who role played as they really are?*

OPTIONAL:
Hand out 3x5 cards and ask people to write the affirmations they need to hear in order to reject destructive messages. Ask them to keep the cards and read the messages five times daily.

---

4. RESPONSIBILITY
(20-25 Minutes)

Ask: *Will someone tell how you*
✳ *encouraged a child to think and feel for himself this week?*

176

Say: *This exercise, called I'll Do It Later, is the fifth exercise on encouraging responsibility in children. It is especially important for children from three to six years of age and for teenagers who are making choices about their identity and deciding what kinds of power to use, misuse, or deny.*

One way to encourage children to be responsible is to model and to expect straight nos after age three. There are often communication mix-ups in families when one person wants a yes or no answer to a question, and the other person refrains from saying no directly but says or does something that really means no. In this exercise we will identify some of the ways in which children say crooked nos. And we will practice ways of encouraging straight communication by asking for straight nos.

Ask: *Will each of you tell one way in which children can say no crooked?*

Write list on board.
EXAMPLES:
"I'm busy," "I didn't hear you," "I forgot," "After I do . . .," "I have too much homework," "I can't," "I'm tired," "I'm sick," gives a dirty look or no response at all, says yes but never does it, doesn't finish, blames someone else, is late, walks away, procrastinates, cries,

has temper tantrum, ignores, gets busy with something else.

Say: *I will give you cards with a question written on one side in red and the crooked no written on the other side in blue.*

Ask: *Will you work in pairs?*
Will the first person read the question or demand that is written in red?
Will the second person read the crooked no answer written in blue?
First person, will you assume that you have heard this response many times before and that you have a familiar exasperated or "oh, sigh" feeling? And will you go for a straight answer?
After the first person gets a straight no or yes answer, will the two of you think of one or two other ways in which you can encourage straight answers in this situation?

OPTIONAL:
Read or role play this with someone.

EXAMPLE 1:
Red: Will you take the garbage out?
Blue: I'll do it later.
Red: Will you take it out before you eat your lunch?
Blue: I'd rather take it out after.
Red: Before lunch—yes or no?
Blue: No.
Red: All right.

EXAMPLE 2:
Red: Did you let the cat out?
Blue: I can't remember.
Red: Did you let the cat out?
Blue: No response.
Red: Please tell me if you let the cat out.
Red: I want to know if you let the cat out.
Red: Will you say, "Yes, I let the cat out," or
"No, I didn't let the cat out"?
Blue: No, I didn't let the cat out.

EXAMPLE 3:
Red: Have you picked up your toys?
Blue: I didn't hear you.
Red: Did you pick up your toys?
Red: I expect you to listen to me and to answer the question.
Red: The question is about toys. Have you picked them up?
Blue: No.
Red: Do it now. I will help you.

Hand out 3x5 cards with the questions or demands written on one side in red and the **crooked nos** written on the other side in blue.[5]

Red: Will you take the garbage out?
Blue: I'll do it later.

Red: Did you let the cat out?
Blue: I can't remember.

Red: Come in the house now.
Blue: No response.

Red: Did you turn the hose off?
Blue: I had to go to the bathroom.

Red: Have you written the thank you to Aunt Sally?
Blue: I just didn't get around to it.

Red: Will you go to the store for me?
Blue: Yes. (then forgets to go)

Red: Will you make the phone call to find out when the shop is open?
Blue: I'm awfully busy.

Red: Have you finished your project?
Blue: I didn't know you wanted it today.

Red: My library book was due yesterday. Did you return it for me?
Blue: I misunderstood.

Red: Have you finished cleaning your room?
Blue: I had to do something more important.

Red: Are you going to set the table tonight?
Blue: Soon.

Red: Do you want a sandwich?
Blue: Maybe later.

Red: Will you come help me now?
Blue: Makes an "oh yuk" face.

Red: Will you come help me now?
Blue: After this TV show is over.

Red: Are you ready for school?
Blue: My stomach hurts.

Red: Did you answer the phone?
Blue: I didn't hear it.

Red: Do you want to come to Bullock's with me?

Blue: I am coming down with a cold.

Red: Do you want to go to a movie tonight?
Blue: I'm getting a headache.

Do the role play.
Reassemble the group after three or four minutes.

Ask: *Will each couple read your question and answer to the whole group and then share two ways in which you can invite a straight answer?*

Say: *Thank you. We have identified some ways children say no crooked and we have practiced alternative ways of inviting straight answers.*

Say: *While you were improving your ability to invite straight answers from children, did you think of some ways in which parents invite crooked nos?*

EXAMPLES of ways to invite crooked nos:
  1. Ask the child, "Will you?" and respond to a no with "That is not the answer I wanted."
  2. Ask, "Will you?" and plead

with the child to change to yes.

3. Ask, "Will you?" when you really mean, "You have to."
4. Ask, "Did you . . .?" in a threatening voice.
5. Punish for a straight no.
6. If the answer is yes, forget to stroke the child when he carries through or forget to impose a penalty if he doesn't.
7. Teach the child that no is an impolite word.
8. Fail to keep your own word with the child.
9. Let the child get by with crooked nos.
10. Use crooked nos yourself.

Say: *Grown-up people who feel like saying no, but don't say it often find other ways of saying no. They may promise to do something and then not do it. The communication skills of asking straight questions and encouraging straight answers are helpful with adults as well as children.*

Ask: *Between now and the next meeting:*
1. Will you listen for ways in which people say no crooked?
2. Will you practice asking for straight nos, especially from three to six year olds who are deciding who they are in relation to other people, and from six to twelve year olds who are deciding what rules they are going to incorporate for

themselves, and from fourteen or fifteen year olds who are recycling no-saying?
3. Will you practice saying calm, quiet, powerful, non-vindictive nos?

5. FOUR WAYS OF PARENTING
(10 Minutes)

Do a Four Ways of Parenting exercise if you have not done one earlier at this meeting. Ask the group to suggest a topic or use one from the text, pages 138-139, or do one on "I am afraid to say no to my children."

OPTIONAL:

6. PARENTING TIPS
(0-10 Minutes)

Hold up the text open at pages 136 and 137.

Ask: *Will you turn to the Parenting Tips in the text, pages 136-137?*

Ask: *Does anyone have a question or comment to share about* ✳ *Parenting Tips or about the readings in Chapter five?*

Ask: *Does anyone want a Suggestion Circle on ways to handle teasing between young children?*

Say: *Section D.2. on page 137 in the text says that adults "will give negative strokes for inappropriate behavior with*

reasons and expectations."
There are examples of these
messages on page 19 in the
text.

Say: *The Don't Do This Because,
Do This Instead exercise[6]
gives us a chance to practice
saying don't in an esteem-
building way.*

Ask: *Will you work in pairs? Will
each pair choose an
inappropriate behavior and
decide how you will say
don't do this, because, do
this instead? You may
choose a behavior or you
may use one of the following
examples:
Five year old wipes his nose
on his shirt.
Three year old squeezes the
hamster hard.
Five year old picks his nose.
Four year old spills his milk.
Three year old whines
whenever he wants
something.
Five year old sticks his
tongue out at Uncle Henry.
Five year old doesn't eat his
vegetables.
Three year old leaves toys on
the steps.*

Reassemble the group into a circle.

Ask: *Will each couple tell the
group what the inappropriate
behavior is and what
esteem-raising negative
stroke you will give it?*

After members of the group have
reported . . .

Say: *Thank you. Those messages
are helpful not only for three
to six year olds but for older
children as well.*

---

7. ADDITIONS

Address any items added during
goal setting.

CLOSING (10 Minutes)

Take care of any business details.
Point to the **Goals** poster and
briefly note the content covered.
Distribute the **Homework** handout,
Meeting 6, page 184 .
Review the things to do before the
next meeting:
1. *Get strokes in all Three Parts of
the Personality.*
2. *Give strokes to all Three Parts of
the Personality of someone,
page 141 in text.*
3. *Practice Rejecting Toxic Strokes
from each part of the
personality.*
4. *Practice the affirmations for
yourself or someone else.*
5. *Practice saying no straight and
asking for straight nos.*
6. *Read Chapter seven and
page 260.*

Ask: *Will someone give me a
positive stroke for the way I
nurture? and one for some
clear thinking I have done?*

*and one for my creativity or
sense of humor?*

Say: *Thank you. Now will you
turn to someone near you
and stroke all three Parts of
the Personality of that
person?*

Ask: *Does anyone have
Resentments or
Appreciations?*

Say: *Thank you. The meeting is
closed. I'll see you at the
next meeting.*

Rejecting Toxic Strokes

Set 1 Sender: You are a bad
person!

Set 1 Rejector:
NS You have no right to talk
to me that way! I am a
worthwhile person and I
don't deserve that!
Rejector:
PS I'll think about that.
"Bad" seems to me to be a
strong word for what I have
done. I'm not sure that your
criticism is helpful to me.
Rejector:
SA Ouch! that hurt; please
be nice to me. (meaning I
am a worthwhile person,
and I don't deserve that)
Rejector:
SA You are growing a wart
on your nose! (meaning I
am a worthwhile person and
I can distract you)

Set 2 Sender: You stink!

Set 2 Rejector:
NS I am a worthwhile
person. I don't deserve to be
called names. You must be
feeling bad about yourself to
attack me.
Rejector:
PS Odor, like sight and
sound, is important in
communication. I observe
that you do not enjoy my
odor.
Rejector:
SA Thanks, I'm on my way

to a "stinky contest," and I
thought you'd never notice!

Set 3 Sender: Why did you do that
terrible thing? You are
awful!

Set 3 Rejector:
NS I don't know why I did
it. (Tone of voice indicates
that I have a right to do
things my way without
explaining.)
Rejector:
PS I don't know why I did it.
(Tone of voice indicates I
will think about my
behavior.)
Rejector:
SA I don't know why I did it.
(Tone of voice indicates that
I will do some things
without reporting to you!)

Set 4 Sender: You want help with
your problem? Listen, your
problems are not important!

Set 4 Rejector:
NS (assertively) My problems
are important to me and I
deserve help.
Rejector:
PS (matter-of-fact tone) I
asked for help with my
problem. Does this mean
you are not going to help
me? If so, I will ask
someone else.
Rejector:

SA (indignantly) I sure don't want to play with you!

Set 5 Sender: Why have you suddenly changed the way you discipline the kids?!!

Set 5 Rejector:
NS I believe I need some new ways of parenting!
Rejector:
PS The situation seemed to me to warrant a different approach.
Rejector:
SA I don't know exactly why! I just felt like it.

Set 6 Sender: Oh! You don't work, you just take care of kids (or babysit).

Set 6 Rejector:
NS I think that taking care of children is a very important and rewarding job. I am capable.
Rejector:
PS The need for child care is increasing as more families have two working parents.
Rejector:
SA Boy! Do I have fun with kids!

Homework

1. Get strokes in all Three Parts of the Personality.
2. Give strokes to all Three Parts of the Personality of someone, page 141 in text.
3. Practice Rejecting Toxic Strokes from each part of the personality.
4. Practice the affirmations for yourself or someone else.
5. Practice saying no straight and asking for straight nos.
6. Read Chapter seven and page 260 in the text.

Notes

1. Rollo May, *Power and Innocence: A Search for the Sources of Violence* (New York: Dell Publishing Co., Inc., 1972).
2. Thanks to Sheila Hartmann for her part in creating the Stroke Buffet exercise.
3. Thanks to Jan Schneider and Claudia Freund for contributing some of the sets for the exercise in Rejecting Toxic Strokes.
4. Thanks to Bernadine Gradous for designing and testing the exercise for review of the Three Parts of the Personality.
5. Thanks to Carole Gesme and class members for these examples. Thanks to the evening Facilitators Support Group for editing the Crooked Nos exercise.
6. Thanks to Marita Erickson for help with the Don't Do This Because—Do This Instead exercise.For further information, see Elizabeth Crary, *Without Spanking or Spoiling* (Seattle: Parenting Press, 1979).

LETTER TO MARJ 7

Dear Marj,

Meeting seven. I expect that by now your group is rolling and that you are feeling competent and comfortable as a facilitator. If you haven't made any mistakes yet, I hope you make one . . . and admit it . . . and repair it. Leaders who never make a mistake don't seem human. Anyway, how else can you model that it is OK for people to make mistakes and grow from them?

Drawing "Me, Right Now" is so much fun as an **opener!** People draw with quiet intensity. When I am working in a carpeted room, I throw the crayons in the middle of the floor, and people often sit on the floor or lie on their stomachs like a bunch of kids, busily coloring. They get and give lots of good strokes during the show-and-tell time, too.

As usual, think about time as you watch and listen for responses to the **Goals.** If several people want to practice Rejecting Toxic Strokes, plan what you will compress, but do not omit the **Stroke Fair.** When you mention planning a celebration for the last meeting, decide whether you will celebrate during the meeting, or before or after the meeting. Also, find out whether this group wants time to consider continuing as a support group. If they do, plan time during Meetings 7 and 8 for that.

l. I love the **Stroke Fair!** I go to each booth and get a whole bunch of strokes! If everyone passed, I would run each booth in turn and stroke myself as well as anyone who came to the booth. Have fun making the banners. Mine were made for me by a member of one of my classes. The Nurturing and Structuring Part banner is soft in color and texture. The words "Nurturing and Structuring" are in the center, and next to them are various words and symbols that represent nurturing, values, and traditions: a small book labeled "Love," a list of rules, a tiny cross, a menorah, a recipe, a fireplace. It even has a tiny fence on it. The Problem Solving Part banner is crisp with orderly letters, lots of numbers and blocks and puzzle pieces. The Spontaneous and Adaptive Part banner is soft and fuzzy. Attached to it are some party favors, pictures of grown-up toys, and a funny birthday card.

Emphasize the idea that, especially after age six, the least developed part of the personality needs the most strokes. It is so easy to compliment people on what they do well that we sometimes forget the importance of complimenting them on what they are starting to do—even clumsily. For some people the exercise of writing strokes to all three parts of the personality (What You Stroke Is What You Get), is the most powerful exercise in any of the meetings!

2. In the exercise **Rejecting Toxic Strokes,** invite people to use their own examples. Move along beside them and encourage them. If someone uses a rejection that is a put-down, I ask other people in the group to suggest alternatives from the same part of the personality. Don't worry if each one isn't exactly correct. My groups usually enjoy this exercise and laugh as they invent silly options.

3. The role play in **Discounting on Four Modes or Levels** can be done very quickly. Urge Pat and Kip to put on a convincing act. Derole carefully, as always. This whole exercise is not very long, but some people make changes in their own behavior as a result of understanding it. Stress the fact that all people may discount on all four levels at some time but that we are responsible for and in charge of our own discounting and we can change our own behavior if we want to.

4. **The Responsibility and Redefinition** exercise is a real mind-blower for some of us, especially if we have been redefining or redefined that very day. Understanding and resisting redefinitions is a powerful tool for settling arguments and encouraging straight communications.

   Sometimes I make the idea of Frame of Reference visible by taking pieces of cardboard and cutting holes of different sizes and shapes in each one. I give a frame to each participant and ask her to write "My mother has a more beautiful voice than I have" on it. Then I say, "You have a beautiful voice." I ask them to tell me how they would redefine me if they were protecting that preconceived notion. When I work with foster parents, I give them cardboard frames, ask them to guess what preconceived notions their foster child may have. Then I ask them to go through the affirmations and look for counter messages.

   The powerful thing about the Redefinition exercise is that you do not have to know what the preconceived notion was. Whenever you counter a redefinition, you invite the child to attend to the present, to accept the love, or to respond to the structure that is present now rather than trying to mold it to fit her preconceived notions.

5. Many of us need at least six weeks practice with new parent tapes or new ways of behaving before we start to *feel* natural. That is why the **Four Ways of Parenting** is practiced at every meeting and is not optional.

6. Ah, who of us does not need **Affirmations for Sexuality and for Separation?** I surely do. My oldest son has left for college; my

daughter is graduating from high school; our visiting Finnish student, Anne Kerttula, is leaving in July; and I am separating from the idea that moms are big people who take care of little people. What does it mean for moms who have lost their jobs of being moms to be "welcome to come home again"? Welcome back into the work force? Professional life? A new career? Back to school? It is an interesting time of life. The opportunities and decisions are parallel to those of late teenage.

7. **Parenting Tips** for parenting the child from thirteen to nineteen years is optional. I certainly do like all these second chances to solve problems. Share your own good experiences and have a good time with this.

8. Think through what role you wish to have if this group decides to continue as a **Support Group.** Preview the section on Support Groups in Meeting 8 in case you get specific questions.

For the **Closing,** find out if people want an exercise repeated at the last meeting so you will know what materials to bring. I ask my groups if they are willing to do Stroke Fair again because I like it. You may look ahead to Meeting 8 and select options now if you want to.

Some groups plan a special celebration with food. They bring coffee and cookies, or have a potluck meal before or after the class, or all go somewhere to eat together. Others plan celebrations with gifts. Each person brings some presents or a game or poem or song to share with the group. Your group may invent a new way to celebrate! Have fun!

Love,

Jean

MEETING 7

BEFORE MEETING 7

1. Study Meeting 7 plan.
2. Reread Chapters seven and nine and pages 262 and 265 in text.
3. Read the seventh Letter to Marj.
4. Reread "Who, Me, Lead a Group?", Question 7.
5. Collect the following **supplies:**
   chalk
   crayons or colored chalk
6. Make or collect the following **visual aids:**

POSTERS
- Meeting 7 Goals, Meeting 7, page 191
   Ground Rules, Meeting 1, page 37
- All six Affirmation posters, Meeting 2, page 63
- Four Modes or Levels of Discounting, Meeting 7, page 194

CARDS AND SIGNS
- Three Parts of Personality banners, Marj 7, page 187
- Cards for Rejecting Toxic Strokes exercise, Meeting 6, pages 182-183
- Five direction cards for Levels of Discounting exercise, Meeting 7, pages 193-194
- Three Parts of Personality circles, Meeting 2, page 92
- Cards for Redefinition exercise, Meeting 7, pages 196-197
- Four Ways of Parenting signs, Marj 1, page 33
- Affirmation cymbals, all six sets

DUPLICATED HANDOUTS
- Me, _____, Right Now, Meeting 7, page 203
- Stroke Fair, Meeting 7, pages 204-205
- Homework, Meeting 7, page 206

OPENING *(10-15 Minutes)*

Post the posters and hang Three Parts of the Personality banners in different parts of the room.
Lay out colored crayons or colored chalk.
Hand "Me, _____, Right Now" sheets to people as they enter and ask them to follow the directions on the sheet.

Ask: *Will you draw a picture of the Three Parts of the Personality showing how you feel right now?*

Lay out all six sets of **affirmation** cymbals and masking tape.
After three minutes . . .

Ask: *Remembering your right to pass, will you show your drawing and tell what it means to you?*

Ask: *Will you select an affirmation cymbal that will help you balance the parts of your personality and tape it to yourself and wear it today? Will you ask someone to read the affirmation to you or will you ask for any other strokes that you want right now?*

GOALS
Point to the **Goals** poster.

```
    MEETING 7 GOALS
    1.  Stroke Fair
    2.  Rejecting Toxic
        Strokes
    3.  Four Modes or
        Levels of
        Discounting
    4.  Responsibility and
        Redefinitions
    5.  Four Ways of
        Parenting
    6.  Affirmations for
        Sexuality and
        Separation
    7.  Parenting Tips
    8.  Support Groups
    9.  Additions
    10. Plan Next Meeting
    11. Celebrations
```

Read and negotiate the Goals:

1. **Stroke Fair** —*We will continue the review of all three parts of the personality with this exercise. Stroke Fair is a way to practice giving and receiving strokes in all three.*
2. **Rejecting Toxic Strokes** —*We will continue practicing this.*
3. **Four Modes or Levels of Discounting** —*We will consider the seriousness of each.*
4. **Responsibility and Redefinitions** —*We will continue to explore ways of inviting children and ourselves to be responsible by identifying and practicing ways to counter redefinitions.*

5. **Four Ways of Parenting** —*We will practice them.*
6. **Affirmations for Sexuality and Separation**—*We will practice them and consider how to offer them to teenagers and to ourselves.*
7. **Parenting Tips**—*Does anyone want time to discuss Parenting Tips on teenagers and blended families?*
8. **Support Groups**—*We will see if people in this group want to continue it as a support group.*
9. **Additions**—*Does anyone have suggestions for topics to be addressed by a Suggestion Circle or a Four Parent?*
10. *We will* **plan** *a Celebration for our* **next meeting.**
11. *Does anyone want to share a* **Celebration?**

1. STROKE FAIR
(5-10 Minutes)

Say: *We all need strokes to all three parts of the personality. We can practice giving and receiving strokes in all three parts by giving them at the Stroke Fair. The three banners represent booths, like booths at a carnival. Here are some examples you can use if you want to.*

Hand out **Stroke Fair,** Meeting 7, pages 204-205
Point to the **Nurturing and Structuring, Problem Solving,** and **Spontaneous and Adaptive** banners in different parts of the room.

Ask: *Will someone give strokes to the **Nurturing and Structuring Part** of other people by standing under the Nurturing and Structuring banner and complimenting people on their nurturing, structuring, protecting skills, and on their beliefs, values, standards, ethics, helpfulness? Use the samples from the handout sheet if you want to.*

*Will someone give strokes to the **Problem Solving Part** of others by standing under the Problem Solving banner and complimenting them on their thinking, problem solving, data gathering or probability estimating skills?*

*Will a third person give strokes to the **Spontaneous and Adaptive Part** of other people by standing under the Spontaneous and Adaptive banner and complimenting others on their creativity, fun, beauty, sparkle, tenderness, boisterousness, sexiness, spontaneity, stubbornness, or rebelliousness?*

Ask: *Will the rest of you move from booth to booth and sample the wares at each?*

After three minutes ask someone else to staff each booth so the people who were giving strokes can have a turn to get strokes. Switch again if the group is large. Reassemble people in a circle.

Ask: *Will someone give special strokes to the people who were giving strokes? Did*

anyone find that it was easier to take strokes in one part of the personality than in another?*

Say: *I urge you to continue accepting positive strokes in all three parts of the personality even if it seems difficult to take them at first. It is all right to feel uncomfortable and awkward while we learn something new. Getting strokes in all three parts of our personality is healthy. One way we can help children to develop all three parts is to stroke all three. The part that is least "strokable" needs the most strokes.*

Ask: *Will someone read the three sets of strokes that you recorded on page 141 since our last meeting?*

Ask: *Will you use page 211 to choose another set of strokes to practice between now and our next meeting?*

2. REJECTING TOXIC STROKES[1]
(10 Minutes)

Ask: *Will those of you who practiced resisting toxic or destructive strokes or discounts report on your successes? Did anybody find new methods? Do any of you want to share the affirmations you said to yourselves about rejecting toxic strokes?*

192

Say: *Children deserve to be taught how to throw away toxic strokes. Will you share some ways in which you are teaching your children to reject toxic strokes?*

Say: *Children are less vulnerable to toxic strokes if they feel lovable and capable.*

Do one or two more sets from the Resisting Toxic Strokes exercise in Meeting 6, page 174, or ask if anyone has a specific destructive message she would like to practice rejecting from all three parts of the personality.

Ask: *Will you stand outside the Parts of the Personality markers and listen to the toxic strokes? Then move to the part of the personality that is most helpful in rejecting that toxic stroke and practice rejecting it.*

3. FOUR MODES OR LEVELS OF DISCOUNTING
(15-20 Minutes)

Ask: *We have talked and read about discounts (pages 116 and 117 in text). Will someone review for us what discounts are?*

OPTIONAL REVIEW:

Say: There are three things that people discount: themselves, others, or situations. Which does each of following discount? "Don't pay any attention to being in a wheelchair—you can do everything the other kids do." (situation)
"Dave won't make a very good father. He grew up without one, you know." (other)
"I was so mad, I couldn't think." (self)

Say: *There are four modes or levels of discounting problems.[2] This exercise shows the four levels. It is a role play about two kids and an adult group leader. It could be a Scout meeting or a school situation.*

Hold up five **role play** cards.

Ask: *Will two of you volunteer to play the roles of two children, Pat and Kip? Kip is a bully and picks on Pat constantly. Pat gets hurt and the activity interrupts the meeting.*

Ask: *Will five of you play the roles of adult leaders who react in different ways? Hold the card with the number side toward the other people and follow instructions on the "direction" side of the card.*

Hand out the numbered cards with the directions and numbers on them:

Card 1   Number side: 1.
Direction side: Walk past Pat and Kip

and do not see them or respond to them.

Card 2   Number side: 2. Direction side: Walk past the kids, say "Hi" and smile at them.

Card 3   Number side: 3. Direction side: Look at the kids, and say, "Those two kids are disrupting the whole group, and one of them is getting hurt, but there is nothing you can do—kids do tease each other."

Card 4   Number side: 4. Direction side: Look at the kids and say, "I can't run this meeting, and one of those kids is getting hurt, but I don't know how to deal with kids this age!"

Card 5   Number side: 5. Direction side: Observe the situation. Walk up to the kids. Separate them. Say, "I expect you to find ways to act that will not disrupt the whole group activity, and I expect nobody to get hurt."

Ask: *Will the person playing the role of the bully, Kip, tease Pat and pretend to hurt her? (The people playing the adult roles do so in any order.)*

Do the role play.

Ask: *Will you go back to your seats, turn in the cards and with the cards your roles? Will you see yourselves as competent, caring people? Will the rest of the group see everyone as they are, and not as the role suggested?*

Collect the cards.

Point to the **Four Modes or Levels of Discounting a Problem** poster.

FOUR MODES OR LEVELS
OF DISCOUNTING
A PROBLEM
1. Existence of problem
2. Significance of problem
3. Solvability of problem
4. Person's ability to solve problem

Say: *There are four modes or levels of discounting a problem. Think about what was said during the role playing.*

Ask: *Which person discounted the **existence** of the problem? (No. 1)*

Say: *The person discounting on this level says, "The stimulus or the problem does not exist."*

Ask: *Which person discounted the seriousness or **significance** of the problem? (No. 2)*

194

Say: *The person who discounts on this level says, "There is a problem, but it's not serious, so I don't have to do anything about it."*

Ask: *Which person discounted the* **solvability** *of the problem? (No. 3)*

Say: *The person discounting on this level says, "Kids will be kids; there is nothing anybody can do."*

Ask: *Which person discounted her* **ability** *to be effective? (No. 4)*

Say: *The person discounting on this level says, "I see that there is a problem, but I am powerless to do anything."*

Ask: *Which person did not discount the problem and took into account both the situation and herself? (No. 5)*

Say: *Discounting at any of the four levels keeps the problem from being solved. Probably everyone discounts at all four levels sometimes. Understanding different levels of discounting helps me make decisions about myself and other people. Frequent discounting at the first and second levels (the existence or the significance of the problem) indicates more serious personality problems than does discounting at the third or fourth levels (the solvability of the problem or the person's ability to solve it.) For example, "What is this stuff about strokes? Nobody needs*

anything like that . . . All you need to do is work hard and keep your nose clean, and that should be enough for anybody in this life" indicates a more serious personality problem than "I can't think of any way to get what I want out of life." If people are consistently discounting at the first and second levels, they can take this as an indicator that they should think about making some changes (taking better care of themselves, finding a healthier support group, or getting some therapy).

OPTIONAL:
If there was no Suggestion Circle at the beginning of the meeting,

Ask: *Do you want a Suggestion Circle on ways to confront destructive teasing or bullying without discounting?*

Say: *Understanding Levels of Discounting can help you select the people you want to do an activity with. Assume that you are looking for someone to help you solve a problem, and everyone you ask discounts it. Do not try to recruit the first and second level discounters. You will be more effective if you go to the fourth level discounters with "Here is something you can do." And to the third level discounters you can say,*

*"Here is how some other
people have solved this
problem, so let's try that."*

Say: *Suppose you are looking for
people to help you get a
stoplight installed at a
hazardous crossing near a
school. Which persons would
you recruit?
Smith: "Well, nobody has
been killed there."
Ursino: "Who, me? I wouldn't
know how to get a stoplight!"
Anderson: "Well, I guess we
could use a light, but you
remember, you can't fight
city hall."
Butorski: "I don't think it's a
hazard."*

Point to **Four Levels of
Discounting** poster.

Ask: *Will you identify the level or
mode of discounting of the
following?*
  - *"So the kid is black and
    blue and you think he has
    been battered? What's so
    bad about that? He's alive,
    isn't he?"* (Seriousness—
    2nd level)
  - *"I can't understand what
    the "Women's Movement" is
    all about. Bunch of
    silliness if you ask me.
    Women have it good. They
    shouldn't complain."*
    (Problem—1st level)
  - *"I would like to lose some
    weight, but I just can't
    seem to."* (Self—4th level)
  - *"We do need better
    facilities for disabled
    persons in our building, but
    after all, we can't tear this*

*place down and build a
whole new building."*
(Solvability—3rd level)

Say: *During the coming week be
aware of the levels of
discounting that you hear.*

4. RESPONSIBILITY AND REDEFINITIONS[3]
(20 Minutes)

Say: *At our last meeting we
practiced recognizing crooked
nos and asking for straight
ones.*

Ask: *Will someone who recognized
✳ a crooked no and got a
straight one tell us how you
did that?*

Say: *The sixth Responsibility
exercise offers us a chance to
recognize and counter
Redefinitions, or ways in
which people change
meanings to avoid
responsibility. It is called
Where Are Your Boots?*

Hand out 3x5 cards with **stimulus
statements** written on one side in
blue and **response statements**
written on the other side in red.

Blue: How much money do
you need?
Red: I don't need it until
later.

Blue: When are you going to
bed?
Red: Why do you ask?

Blue: How did you get the hole in your shirt?
Red: I'm going to wear another shirt today.

Blue: Where are your boots?
Red: I'm not going to wear them today.

Blue: What does my visit to your house have to do with your problem?
Red: I was thinking about that this morning.

Blue: Do you like my new coat?
Red: Where did you get it?

Blue: I hear you did a great job. How did you get started?
Red: I always do a great job.

Blue: Let's get a pizza.
Red: I ate a lot at the movies.

Blue: When is it convenient for you to come?
Red: When is it OK with you?

Blue: What kind of painting do you like to do best?
Red: Whatever pleases people.

Blue: Thank you for being so patient. What would you like to do now?
Red: Have you teach me how to be patient.

Ask: *Will you work in pairs? Will one of you read the blue side and the other respond with the statement on the red side? Will the blue side person not respond back immediately? Think about how you feel and then say a word to describe your feelings.*

After people have read their cards, get their attention but have them stay in pairs.

Ask: *Will each blue side person tell the whole group your feeling word?*

Go around the circle quickly, getting one or two feeling words from each person.

Say: *A person redefines when, in response to a statement or question, she switches the context of the original message. For example, she may switch from "how" to "what," "when" to "where," or "who" to "why." One can also redefine by switching from one "what" to another "what" or from one "how" to another "how."*

Ask: *Will each couple identify their switch to each other?*
EXAMPLE:
Where are your boots? (where)
I'm not going to wear them today. (when)
After about two minutes, get the group's attention.

Ask: *Will each couple read both sides of their card to the whole group and identify the switch?*

Ask: *Working in pairs again, will you reread the blue and red sides as written? Then will the blue person repeat the stimulus until the question is answered or the response is relevant?*

EXAMPLE:
Where are your boots?
I'm not going to wear them today.
Where are they?
I told you I don't need them today.
OK, you don't need them today, where are they today?
Why does it matter?
I want to know. Will you tell me?
I left them at Lee's house.

After three minutes . . .

Ask: *Will several of you describe the feelings you had when you got straight answers compared with the feelings you had when you were redefined?*

Say: *Redefinition is a way in which people turn or alter stimuli to fit their frame of reference, their preconceived notions of themselves, other people, and the world.*
EXAMPLE:
Sally's preconceived notion was that her mother was important because she had a beautiful voice and that Sally was not important and did not have a beautiful voice, even though she did.
"Sally, you have a beautiful voice."
"You should have heard my mother's voice."
By redefining the incoming data about her voice, Sally maintained her original position (her Frame of Reference) that her mother

was more important than she was.

Redefining discounts the sender because she doesn't get a straight answer. And the redefiner discounts herself because she alters her importance or reality. When people take responsibility for their own stroke economy, for getting adequate strokes of the kinds they want, they stop redefining and discounting their own stroke needs, and they do not internalize discounts from other people.

Ask: *Will you listen for and counter Redefinitions before the next meeting?*

5. FOUR WAYS OF PARENTING *(10 Minutes)*

Do the Four Ways of Parenting exercise.
Use a situation from the group or one from pages 204 and 205 in the text.

6. AFFIRMATIONS FOR SEXUALITY AND SEPARATION
(15-20 Minutes)

Ask: *Does anyone have any beliefs, thoughts or feelings to share about giving and getting the affirmations? Did* anyone invent a new way of using them?

Say: *Affirmations for Sexuality and Separation are important for thirteen- to nineteen-year-old persons, for any older persons who are making relationship separations or examining their sexuality, and for everyone else over twelve years of age.*

Point to and read the **Affirmations for Sexuality and Separation** poster:

AFFIRMATIONS FOR
SEXUALITY AND
SEPARATION
You can be a sexual person
and still have needs.
It's OK to be responsible
for your own needs, feelings,
and behavior.
It's OK to be on your own.
You're welcome to come
home again.
My love goes with you.

Say: *These are some of the messages that people from thirteen to nineteen years of age need to hear. This is the time during which people recycle old problems and needs with the added dimension of sexuality. It is a time for separating from parents and assuming responsibility for self. These messages are helpful during the many separations that occur following adolescence.*

Ask: *Will you listen to these affirmations in different*

ways? *Think of a specific teenager, pretend you are that person, and listen to the messages:*

- *"You can be a sexual person and still have needs. Sexual people get mad and sad and scared and need nurturing.*
- *It's important to know who you are. You can become the person you want to be, and you can be responsible for yourself. You don't need to be a carbon copy of me or of anyone else.*
- *You're welcome to come home again.*
- *You may need space away from me while we are separating, but I look forward to knowing you as an adult, an equal . . . I love you."*

Ask: *Will you stop pretending to be a teenager, let go of any negative feelings you may have had while pretending, and be yourselves now? And decide whether any message sounded especially helpful. Which one?*

Ask: *Will you pretend you have just lost something or someone—a job, a loved person, an opportunity, a capability, a part of your body—and listen again? "You can be a grownup and competent and still have needs. It's desirable to ask other people for help and comfort. It's important to know who you are. You may have had some of your* identity tied up in whatever your loss was related to, such as being a lover, parent, son or daughter, teacher, athlete, boss. You may feel empty right now, but you can look forward to feeling whole again. You are significant because you are you. You are welcome to fully reenter society in your new role as soon as you are ready. You may not think so now, but you will be a deeper, bigger person because of this experience . . . I love you."

Ask: *Will you leave the role play? Leave behind any sad or negative feelings you may have had while you were thinking about a loss. Come back to being who you are in the present.*

Ask: *Do any of you want to tell what changes would make these messages more effective for you?*

Turn to the Affirmations for Sexuality and Separation, pages 206 and 207 in the text, and ask people to compare them to the ones on the poster.
Remind people that if they need any of these messages they can ask someone to give them. There may be people in this group who will give these affirmations to each other.

Say: *Practice giving and getting these messages before the next meeting.*

Ask: *Will you write in the*

affirmations the way you want to hear them on page 207, and will you give them to someone else before the next meeting?

OPTIONAL:
7. PARENTING TIPS
(10 Minutes)

Turn to the Parenting Tips for Raising the Thirteen- to Nineteen-Year-Old Child, page 203 in the text.

Ask: *Does anyone have any thoughts or questions about these Parenting Tips or about Chapter seven?*

Say: *This exercise will give us the chance to think what it is like to be a teenager and to think about how her world differs from that of an older generation.*

Ask: *Will you work in pairs? Will you interview your partner and find out what were the most significant events in her life the year she was sixteen?*

After about three minutes, reassemble the group in a circle.

Ask: *Will each of you report what were the most important events in your partner's life the year she was sixteen?*

Ask: *Will you work in pairs again and tell each other what parents or other significant adults in your life did that* helped you through the journey of a sixteen year old or what you wish they had done?

After about three minutes . . .

Ask: *If you were sixteen right now, in today's world situation, what parts of the positive parenting that you just described would you want? What would you want or need that is different from what you described?*

Ask: *Will each of you share one thing that you admire about some specific teenager you know?*

---

8. SUPPORT GROUPS
(3 Minutes)

Say: *Sometimes people who have been together in a learning group like this one choose to continue to meet as a support group.*

Ask: *Are there any of you who think you would like to do that?*

Ask: *Will all of you think about it before the next meeting? We will talk about how a support group might work and how to form one. You may already have experience with support groups, and there is information about kinds of support in Chapter nine in the text, "The Care and Feeding of Support Groups."*

9. ADDITIONS

Address any items added during goal settings.

10. PLAN NEXT MEETING

Plan a Celebration for the closing meeting.
Select Options for Meeting 8 at this time if you want to.
Select any exercises from the previous meetings that you may want repeated during Meeting 8.

CLOSING

Point to the **Goals** poster and note content covered.
Take care of any business details.
Distribute the homework handout and review the homework for the next meeting:
1. *Do the What You Stroke Is What You Get exercise on page 211 of the text.*
2. *Listen for Redefinitions and practice countering them in a variety of ways.*
3. *During the coming week be aware of the Levels of Discounting that you hear.*
4. *Give the Affirmations for Separation and Sexuality to yourself and to someone who is thirteen to nineteen years old.*
5. *Read Chapters eight and nine in the text.*

Ask: *Does anyone have any Resentments? Appreciations?*

Say: *Will you get two people to give you the affirmation you chose at the start of the meeting, and then will you leave the Affirmation cymbals on the table?*

Say: *Thank you. The meeting is closed. I'll see you at our next (and last) meeting.*

Me, _____ , Right Now

Draw a picture of your Three Parts of the Personality right now.
Maybe one part is large and smooth and feeling good. Maybe one is
shrunken or rumpled. Maybe one is smiling. Maybe one is
growing.

Are there any kinds of strokes that you need? Will you ask for them?

Stroke Fair
Examples of Strokes to the
Three Parts of the Personality

NURTURING AND STRUCTURING PART:

1. I respect your opinion on _____.
2. I admire your ethical stand on _____.
3. I like the way you protected _____.
4. Will you please criticize this drawing for me?
5. Your criticisms are so harsh I have trouble hearing them.
6. You control your dog well. (Also temper, irritation, wish to "fix" other people)
7. I admire the way you organize _____.
8. Your drawer (desk top, toybox) is very neat.
9. You take good care of your clothes. (children, pets, business, house)
10. I respect your judgment about _____.
11. You are a very warm, loving, nurturing person.
12. I love to watch the way you hold your baby.
13. You took good care of Jimmy when he was hurt.
14. Your insistence on getting help for yourself and your family when you needed it is something you can be proud of.
15. You are a very supportive person.
16. Thank you for helping me.
17.
18.

PROBLEM SOLVING PART:

1. You are a good problem solver.
2. You think well.
3. That is a workable decision.
4. You did a nice job of finding out that information.
5. You are smart.
6. You do a good job of taking all the aspects of a problem into account.
7. Will you give me some information about _____?
8. You do a good job of figuring out what you need.
9. You allow yourself to know what you want.
10.
11.

SPONTANEOUS AND ADAPTIVE PART:

1. You are fun to be with.
2. You are creative.
3. You're so clever!
4. You're cute!
5. Wow! You are great.
6. You followed those instructions very well.
7. You have perfect manners!
8. How can you sit back and take that?
9. You are a rebellious one!
10. Tell me about your wishes—you make them sound so pretty.
11. Tell me one of those stories you make up.
12. You certainly are mad!
13. I enjoy your curiosity.
14. You sure are a tricky kid!
15. Got any hunches about this?
16. Let's play!
17. I want you to come to my party.
18.
19.

Homework

1. Do the What You Stroke Is What You Get exercise on page 211 of text.
2. Listen for Redefinitions and practice countering them in a variety of ways.
3. During the coming week be aware of the Levels of Discounting you hear.
4. Give the Affirmations for Sexuality and Separation to yourself and to someone who is thirteen to nineteen years old.
5. Read Chapters eight and nine in text.

Notes

1. Thanks to Shirley Bullock for clarifying the exercise Rejecting Toxic Strokes.
2. Jacqui Schiff, *Cathexis Reader* (New York: Harper & Row, 1975).
3. Thanks to Lexi Cummings for helping to clarify the exercise on Redefinitions.

LETTER TO MARJ 8

Hey Marj!
This is the last meeting—congratulations—I knew you could do it!
This meeting is loose—sometimes people take a lot of time for Four
Ways of Parenting or Suggestion Circles. Sometimes while they
review individual goals they take a leisurely trip back through the
meetings, assessing growth, celebrating wins and setting new
goals. Sometimes they zing on to the Optional Exercises and insist
on doing three or more. It is their meeting. Your responsibility is
to help them claim their wins, get the feedback *you* need, and
make sure the group experiences closure.

If you negotiated the **Goals** at the last meeting, post them
and go! Otherwise negotiate now. Hear the wishes of the people!
When you present the **Optional Exercises** you can give a one
sentence description of each, or you could personalize it and say,
"I like doing the Five Dot Exercise because it is fun to hear what
other people think I do well."

1. Listen to the **Review of Individual Goals** and celebrate! Don't
   forget to include your own goals.
2. Honor the **Homework.** Sometimes people share their most
   important learnings while they modestly report doing some
   assigned task. If people seem to want more time on affirmations,
   do more. Ask them to invent a way to share the affirmations. Or
   do an Affirmation Fair. Spread the affirmations on a table or on
   the floor and ask each person to pick up messages he is
   comfortable giving. Use masking tape to stick the messages on
   people. Then ask each person to find the person wearing each
   affirmation he wants to hear and to ask for it.
3. When I am coteaching, my coworker and I sometimes offer an
   Options Fair. We each do two twenty-minute exercises
   simultaneously. This gives people four options from which to
   choose. Other times one or more of the group members will
   prepare and give one or two of the Options.
   Option A—Forming an ongoing support group. Some groups
   do, some don't. You have fulfilled your contract with the group.
   If you join the support group, be clearly a member and don't
   become group parent, or be clearly the leader and get paid.
   Otherwise, you can end up feeling exploited. I try to meet with
   ongoing groups whenever I can because I get so many good
   strokes, but I have a clear contract before the meeting—"I am
   coming for fun," or "May I lead one new twenty-minute exercise
   on self-esteem?" Good Luck!

Option B—The Five Dot activity. This builds strength in a group and in each individual. It is based on the idea that a group is stronger if the people in it have well-balanced personalities and if it does not channel each person into limited roles. I am sure that you will recognize this as an exercise that combines the three Personality Parts we have studied. When I am working with organizations, I refer to structuring as "organizing" and use the word "compromising" to indicate a healthy, grown-up aspect of adaptiveness. Move it quickly. Often my groups insist that we continue it until each person has been included.

Option C—Self-Esteem Today. Winners are people who realize their potential, become what they are capable of becoming, are self-actualized, or whatever else you want to call people who let all their branches blossom. When people are suggesting alternatives for "Reject," I point out that self-esteem rejections do not discount other people.

Emphasize at the end that they are to *appreciate* the positive parts of themselves, not berate themselves for being less than perfect.

Option D—Rejecting Toxic Strokes. This can be done rather quickly. Do not offer it toward the end of the session. Focus on exercises with positive strokes toward the end. One time when Annette Pattie did this exercise, she wrote the same toxic on each slip, "You are a lazy, dumb, worthless person." The exercises that some said helped them to reject that one message were: Centering, the cold, icy stare from the Interaction exercise, Affirmations for Structure, the rebellious part of the Spontaneous and Adaptive Part, the Affirmation It's OK to know who you are, Nurturing and Structuring Part, Frame of Reference, and Ground Rules. Fantastic, I say!

Option E—Extended Stroke Base. This is not intended to imply that strokes from special persons are not important. It is meant to look at how we limit our stroke intake when we insist that one special person supply most of the goodies. What is a reasonable amount? That is up to the Problem Solving Part of each person to decide. I believe that a person who expects over 30% of his strokes from a special person will exploit that person. Not fair!

Options F and G—Four Ways of Parenting and the **Suggestion Circle.** Don't neglect them. You could do either on the question, "How can I continue to get support after this group ends?"

Encourage the group to choose what it wants to do. Members do not all have to do the same things—more than one activity can go on at one time. Offer to repeat an early exercise such as the Three Balloon sheet, the Jelly Bean exercise, Stroke Fair, any of the Responsibility exercises, any of the Affirmations.

4. Read the **Evaluations** later. Savor the good strokes and use the information to build a better course next time. Yes, still Resentments and Appreciations!

5. During the **Multicolored Daisy Celebration,** may your petals curl with joy! Do whatever the group planned at the previous meeting for celebration. I can hardly wait to hear from you!

Love,

Jean

MEETING 8

BEFORE MEETING 8

1. Study Meeting 8 plan.
2. Reread Chapters seven and eight in text.
3. Read the eighth Letter to Marj.
4. Reread "Who, Me, Lead a Group?", Question 8.
5. Collect the following **supplies**:
   three-inch colored circles—one for each person
   one large sheet of paper for each person (16" x 24")
   masking tape
   felt pens
   several containers of paste or glue
6. Make or collect the following **visual aids**:

POSTERS
- Meeting 8 Goals, Meeting 8, page 213
- Ground Rules, Meeting 1, page 37
- Possible Goals of Ongoing Support Group, Meeting 8, page 214

CARDS AND SIGNS
- Multicolored three-inch long daisy petals—about one dozen for each person
- Four Parent signs, Marj 1, page 33
- Five twelve-inch circles with the following terms written on them: "Nurturing," "Organizing," "Problem Solving," "Creating," and "Compromising" (one term on each side)

DUPLICATED HANDOUTS
- List of exercises, Meeting 8, pages 222-223
- Support Group Meeting, Meeting 8, page 224
- Extended Stroke Base, Meeting 8, page 225
- Evaluation sheet, Meeting 8, page 227

OPENING (10 Minutes)

Post all the posters.
Hand out three-inch colored circles and felt pens.

Ask: *Will you write your name and two positive things about yourself on your name tag?*

After three minutes . . .

Ask: *Will you tell the person next to you the two positive things you wrote and where your Stroke Bank level is? Will you introduce the person next to you and tell where his Stroke Bank level is, the positive things he wrote about himself, and add a few that you have observed?*

GROUND RULES
Point to the **Ground Rules** poster.

Ask: *Will someone say how you think these meetings would have been different if we had not used these Ground Rules?*

GOALS

Points to the **Goals** poster.

```
MEETING 8 GOALS
1. Review Individual
   Goals
2. Homework
3. Options
   A. Support Groups
   B. Five Dot Exercise
   C. Self-Esteem Today
   D. Rejecting Toxic
      Strokes
   E. Extended Stroke
      Base
   F. Four Ways of
      Parenting
   G. Suggestion Circle
   H. Additions
4. Evaluation of
   Meetings
5. Multicolored Daisy
   Celebration
```

Review or set the Goals for the meeting:

1. *Review Individual Goals*—We will look at those from Meetings 1 and 5.
2. *Homework*—We will collect thoughts and feelings about this from the last meeting.
3. *Options*—We will select from the following:
   A. *Support Group*—We will see whether people want to continue this group as a support group. We can plan the first meeting.
   B. *The Five Dot Exercise*—We will use this to pull together the Personality Parts for strong people and strong groups.

C. *Self-Esteem Today*—We can assess our present self-esteem level.
D. *Rejecting Toxic Strokes*—We will pull tools from all the meetings to practice Rejecting Toxic Strokes internally and externally.
E. *Extended Stroke Base*—We will see how to build one and why one is important.
F. *Four Ways of Parenting*—We will see if anyone wants one.
G. *Suggestion Circle*—Does anyone have suggestions for this exercise?
H. *Additions*—We will see if anyone wants to add anything.
4. *Evaluation of Meetings*—I will ask you to fill out an evaluation sheet.
5. *Daisy Celebration*—We will close our meeting with this.

1. REVIEW OF INDIVIDUAL GOALS
(15-20 Minutes)

Ask each person:
> Did you meet your goals for the course? Refer to the goals indicated at the first meeting and updated at Meeting 5, page 142.

If some goals are unmet use a Suggestion Circle or the Four Ways of Parenting or refer the person to another class or group. Or choose an Optional Exercise for this meeting that may help him meet his goals.

2. HOMEWORK
(5-15 Minutes)

Ask: *Do any of you have thoughts, feelings, or questions about the homework you have done since the last meeting?*
What You Stroke Is What You Get, page 211 in text
Recognizing and countering Redefinitions
Modes or Levels of Discounting
Affirmations for Sexuality and Separation
Chapter eight.
What concepts in these meetings do you believe are most helpful for people who abuse chemicals?

3. OPTIONS

OPTION A: FORMING AN ONGOING SUPPORT GROUP
(15-20 Minutes)

Say: *In Chapter nine you read about the importance of support groups.*

Ask: *How many of you belong to a support group right now?*

Point to the **Support Group Goals** poster.

Say: *Here are possible goals for an ongoing support group. We can use them to start thinking about our goals.*

GOALS OF AN
ONGOING SUPPORT
GROUP

1. To get and give positive strokes
2. To get and give criticism as a gift
3. To continue to practice skills learned during the meetings
4. To share wins and suggestions about personal and family growth and problems
5. To learn new information and skills for personal growth and for improving interrelationships in families.
6.
7.
8.

Ask: *How many of you are interested in each goal? What other goals are you interested in adding?*

Say: *If the members are interested in fewer than three common goals, let us not continue to meet. It is important that people not meet for class reunions and fill the time with small talk, because that invites people back into the stroke rules that they used before they came to the class.*

If several people are interested in three or more of the goals . . .

Ask: *How many want to form a support group?*

Say: *If the group elects to continue, unless you are going to pay a professional leader, it is important to share the responsibility for planning the meetings. In some groups, each member takes a turn being host, and as host, plans the whole meeting. Other groups have one person act as host and another plan content. In either case, make a clear contract among yourselves about who is responsible for planning content for each meeting. If people want to "just talk," don't meet. The purpose of a support group is to help people maintain their gains and make new growth. If "just talk" would accomplish that, people would not have come to this group in the first place. If people want to have a party, plan it that way. A positive stroke activity for the opening of the meeting and another for the closing are important. When stroke levels rise during the meeting, the support group is functioning properly. If the stroke levels fall, change the activities or stop meeting. Remember, the purpose of the course is for individual members to get their needs met and to learn more about living with other people.*

If the group wants to continue meeting, hand out the **Support Group Meeting** planning sheet (Meeting 8, page 224) and plan the first meeting.

OPTION B: FIVE DOT EXERCISE[1] *(10 Minutes)*

Place on the floor circles with the words "Nurturing," "Organizing," "Problem Solving," "Creating" and "Compromising."

Say:*Five skills that are needed in any group are nurturing, organizing, compromising, problem solving and creating. These skills involve all of the personality parts.*

●Say:*Let us identify some of the strengths in our group. Since every group needs people who are supportive nurturers, people who take good care of other individuals and who take care of the group, will you tell me the name of one person here who does a good job of nurturing?*

Ask the person identified:
Will you come and stand on the Nurturing dot? (If more than one person is identified, choose one and hold the second name for a later rerun of the activity.)

●Say:*Every group needs people who are good at organization, at providing structure. Who in this group has strong organizational skills?*

Ask the person identified:
Will you stand on the Organizing dot?

215

- Say: *When we have a problem we need a good problem solver. Who in this group is good at solving problems?*

Ask the person identified:
Will you stand on the Problem Solving dot?

- Say: *The ability to compromise, to pour oil on troubled waters, is important to a group. Who here do you look to for help when we need to be able to compromise?*

Ask the person identified:
Will you stand on the Compromising dot?

- Say: *Without creativity and spontaneity, a group would be lifeless and not very much fun. Who offers creativity in this group?*

Ask the person identified:
Will you stand on the Creating dot?

Say: *Here we see people who help us create a strong group, people who have developed skills that we appreciate. However, if we allow ourselves to slip into the habit of always calling on the same people to do the same jobs, we limit our group and ourselves. If we depend only on one problem solver, what will we do if we have a problem and that person is unavailable? Also, we are cheating ourselves as individuals if we put each other into "expertise slots" and don't expect each other to grow. I will show one way*

in which we can encourage each other. Go to each person in turn and ask him to claim the competent behavior that the group has identified.

Then ask:
Is there an area indicated by one of the other dots in which you are not as strong? Will you move and stand on that dot? When all five people have claimed their strength and then moved to a dot that identifies an area in which they are less strong, go to each person in turn and ask the group to identify a specific incident in which that person has been successful in that area.
EXAMPLE:
To Aaron, who moved from Compromising to Organizing, say, "Aaron, we know that you are good at helping us compromise and we appreciate that. Now you tell us that you may not have strong organizational skills. Will someone in the group tell Aaron about a time when he organized well, or provided good structure, or suggested a workable procedure when you needed it?"

Encourage the group to give one or two examples and then say. "Aaron, will you accept that you have organizational skills and that we need and appreciate those skills also?"

Repeat for each person.
Repeat the whole activity until every person has been included, if that is what the group wants.

216

Say: *If we form a support group,
this activity could be
repeated every few months to
give people the opportunity to
claim their growing skills
and to observe which
strengths the rest of the group
is currently recognizing in
them. This exercise provides
a way to remind us that we
can build a strong group and
strong individuals by helping
people develop a wide
variety of talents.*

OPTION C:
SELF-ESTEEM TODAY
(20 Minutes)

Ask: *Will you turn to page 176 in
the text?*

Say: *This exercise will give a self-
esteem measure for each of
us for today, not tomorrow
and not yesterday. It will
remain private. It is
personal.*

Say: *Look at the column on the far
right titled "believe." Fill in
other words by the first
balloon. For example, people
who ask for what they want
and need may believe:
I should ask*
    or
I deserve what I need.
    or
I am important.
    or
I have a right to ask.
    or
I can get what I need.
    or

*If I don't get what I ask for
from one person, I can ask
someone else.*

Ask: *Will you write and share
options for each of the next
four actions?*

OPTIONAL EXAMPLES:
Accept: I need healthy
             strokes.
             I deserve strokes.
             It's OK to accept
             strokes.
Give: My strokes are
             important.
             The more I give the
             more I get.
             I won't run out.
Reject: I can decide what I
             need.
             I respect myself as
             much as other
             people.
             I don't have to
             accept destructive
             strokes.
Love: I am lovable.
             It's OK to love
             myself.
             I'm important.
             I'm the best me
             there is.
             I can't love other
             people well if I don't
             love myself first.

Say: *Probably none of us is ever
all in the High Self-Esteem
column or all in the Low
Self-Esteem column. We will
look at where we are now.*

Ask: *Will you fill in the middle
column telling what you do
and what you believe today?*

After about four minutes . . .

Say: *After you have finished filling in your actions and your beliefs for all five items, will you close your eyes and appreciate all the things that you have done in your life to allow you to acquire this positive self-esteem that you have today? Will you think of changes you can make in how you give and get strokes that will raise your own self-esteem?*

OPTION D: REJECTING TOXIC STROKES *(10 Minutes)*

Say: *This exercise on Rejecting Toxic Strokes internally and externally encourages us to draw upon all the techniques and theories we have learned to help us reject toxic messages internally and externally.[2]*

Hand out the exercise sheet.

Ask: *Will you glance at the list of exercises to help you remember the different tools that we have practiced using during these meetings?*

Say: *I will hand you a poisonous message and you are to reject it internally and externally.*

Ask: *Will you look at your poisonous message?*

Say: *Ask yourself if you believe it. Ask yourself if you accept it*

or reject it. *Think about the tools you have acquired during these meetings and from studying* Self-Esteem: A Family Affair *that help you to reject this toxic stroke from the inside and the outside.*

Offer a folded slip of paper with a toxic message written on it to each person. Remind the group of the right to pass.

EXAMPLES OF TOXIC MESSAGES:

You are a lazy, worthless person.
You never do anything right.
You couldn't solve a problem if you met one on the street.
You do pretty well for somebody from your background.
Your contributions have been low quality.
You are irresponsible and overbearing.
You are boring.
You were almost helpful during these meetings.
I think you almost got the message.
You needed this, but I'm not sure it took.
Your lack of effort has been astounding.
Let me think this through for you.

Say: *This is a practice session for Rejecting Toxic Strokes. You can reject the one on the paper, or you can write one you would rather practice rejecting.*

After a minute . . .

Ask: *Will each of you tell us what*

the toxic message was, tear it up, and reject it verbally? After you reject it verbally will you identify which special tools you learned that help you to Reject Toxic Strokes internally?

After people are through rejecting strokes . . .

Say: *Congratulations.*

Ask: *Will you keep your list of exercises to refer to when you fill in your evaluation sheet?*

OPTION E: EXTENDED STROKE BASE[3] *(10-15 Minutes)*

Say: *This exercise is designed:*
  - *to give a person the opportunity to discover that he may unknowingly be expecting a special person to meet an unreasonable number of demands.*
  - *to show that one does not have to give up some needs and wishes just because the special person can't or won't meet them.*
  - *to identify a "service structure," that is, a group of people other than the special person who can help meet needs.*

Hand out the **Extended Stroke Base** sheet.

Ask: *Will each person fill in the left-hand column?*
  EXAMPLE:
  Spouse, relatives, mother,

neighbors, friends, babysitters, church, clubs, school, study groups, welfare agencies, Red Cross, YWCA, YMCA, doctor.

After about two minutes . . .

Ask: *Will each of you share one or two items from your list?*

Say: *Fill in the second column. Any item is OK. This list is private: you will not be asked to share or show this list.*
  EXAMPLE:
  Adequate housing, sex, love, acceptance, strokes, knowledge of how to raise children, intellectual stimulation, entertainment, dancing, snazzy clothes.

Say: *In column three write the name of the "most preferred source" for each need or want. For example: spouse, church, boss, friend.*

Say: *In column four indicate an alternate source for half the "need and want" items.*

Say: *Check the items you can supply for yourself in column five.*

Say: *Look at the "most preferred source" in column three and count the number of times each name appears.*

Ask: *If you have a special person listed several times in column three, will you look at the sources listed in the first column and think of ways to expand your stroke base?*

219

OPTIONAL:
Review the Stroke Rules exercise, pages 76-79 in the text. A rule that you must get most of your needs met by one special person can contribute to a low Stroke Bank level on the days when that person is not available. Also, it may put a very heavy burden on that chosen person.

Ask: *Will you take your list home and consider other ways of being responsible for and to your whole range of stroke sources?*

OPTION F: FOUR WAYS OF PARENTING *(5-10 Minutes)*

Do a Four Parent on a topic suggested by someone in the group or use one from pages 231, 232 or 254, 255 in the text.

OPTION G: SUGGESTION CIRCLE
(3 Minutes)

Do a Suggestion Circle requested by someone in the group or do one on the question, "How can I get support when I feel depressed?"

OPTION H: ADDITIONS

Ask: *Is there any exercise we have done in earlier meetings that you would like to repeat? Does anyone want to add anything?*

4. EVALUATION OF MEETINGS
(10 Minutes)

Hand out copies of the **Evaluation** sheet and ask people to fill them in and leave them with you.
When people have finished writing . . .

Ask: *Does anyone want to share Resentments today? Appreciations?*

5. MULTICOLORED DAISY CELEBRATION[4]
(15-20 Minutes)

Pass a sheet of paper to each person.

Ask: *Will you glue your name tag circle to the middle of the paper to become the center of your daisy?*

Ask: *Will each of you take daisy petals and write on them Affirmations, Appreciations, and Positive Strokes for the other people? Sign your name to the petals if you wish. Give the petals to the other people.*

220

Say: *Glue the petals you receive to your daisy.*
Toss dozens of colored petals toward the ceiling.
After about ten minutes . . .

Ask: *Will you read your own daisy messages to yourselves?*

Say: *It is hard to say "hellos" unless we have said appropriate "good-byes." Even if the people in this group will continue to see each other, it is important to say "good-bye" to these people in this experience.*

Say: *Please move about and say your "good-byes" and Appreciations to people for this particular series of meetings.*

Exercises

Affirmations and Parenting Tips

Being: 0-6 months
Doing Things: 6-18 months
Thinking: 18 months-3 years
Power and Identity: 3-6 years
Structure: 6-12 years
Sexuality and Separation: 13-19 years

Stroke Exercises

Three Balloon Sheet
Five Balloon Sheet
Interaction Exercise
Jelly Bean Exercise
Converting Strokes
Stroke Rules
Stroke Bank Exercise
Stroke Quotient Exercise
Rejecting Strokes Centered and Uncentered
Separating Sex and Nurturing
Stroke Buffet
Rejecting Toxic Strokes from all Three Parts of the Personality
Stroke Fair
Rejecting Toxic Strokes Internally and Externally
Self-Esteem Today
Extended Stroke Base
Daisy Celebration

Framework Exercises

Name Tags
Four Ways of Parenting
Suggestion Circle
Ground Rules
Resentments and Appreciations

Communication Exercises

Back-to-back Interview
Eye Level Exercise
Communicating Centered and Uncentered

Three Parts of the Personality

Nurturing and Structuring (Good Mothers and Good Fathers list)
Problem-Solving (Centering)
Spontaneous and Adaptive Responses (Hug your Aunt Mable)

Discounting and Responsibility

Three Areas of Discounting

Four Modes or Levels of
   Discounting

Asking Straight
   (Your Eggs Are Getting Cold)

People Are Responsible for
   Behavior (Things Are Falling
   into Place)

You are Not Responsible for
   My Feelings (Eat Your Beans
   for Mommy)

I Will Not Think and Feel for
   You (You are Going to Love
   This)

Saying No Straight
   (I'll Do It Later)

Redefinition
   (Where Are Your Boots? I'm
   Not Going to Wear Them
   Today.)

Support Group Meeting[5]

Place _____ Date _____

Host _____

Program _____

Opening Stroke activity

Ground Rules

Sharing wins and problems (Four Ways of Parenting and

Suggestion Circle)

Practice skills, new learnings, play

Plan the next meeting

Closing Stroke activity

Resentments and Appreciations

Extended Stroke Base

1. Parenting help and good strokes. List all the sources of help for parents that I can think of.	2. List all the things that I need or want to help me to be a good parent and a happy person.	3. Most preferred source	4. Alternate source	5. Could do it myself

Extended Stroke Base

1. Parenting help and good strokes. List all the sources of help for parents that I can think of.	2. List all the things that I need or want to help me to be a good parent and a happy person.	3. Most preferred source	4. Alternate source	5. Could do it myself
Friends Relatives Spouse Neighbors Church Social Workers PTA TV Adult classes Magazines Books Radio Pediatrician Organized Support Groups Lectures Baby sitters or Day Care	Help with discipline	Spouse Parents Magazine	Friends Classes Books	
	Understanding children: Is he in a "stage"?	Neighbor	Relatives Classes Books	
	Help with the kids — need some time off.	Relatives	Neighbors Babysitter Day Care	
	Need to be recognized for being me + not just as the parent of some one.	Spouse Relatives	Friends	✓
	Help with the driving	Neighbors	Start a car pool.	
	Information about Children's illnesses	Pediatrician	Nurse Books	
	Feeling good about myself and my kids.			✓

Evaluation[6]

1. My expectations for the session were:

2. I learned that:

3. As a result of the sessions, I plan to change my behavior in these two ways:

4. The two session activities or experiences which I would rate most valuable are:

5. The two session activities or experiences which I would rate least valuable are:

6. The areas to which I would like more attention given are:

7. I would rate the sessions as a whole as:

   0 1 2 3 4 5 6 7 8 9 10

   poor   excellent

8. Two ways I contributed to the group tasks:

9. My participation level for the session was:

   0 1 2 3 4 5 6 7 8 9 10

   passive   very high

10. My goals were, were not met.

11. Strokes for the leaders:

Self-Esteem: A Family Affair Leader Guide, © 1981, Winston Press, Inc.
Permission is given to reproduce this page for classroom use.

Notes:

1. Thanks to Sally Dierks, Harold Miller, and Richard McDonald for helping to design the Five Dot Group Strength Building Exercise. This exercise is adapted from *We*, a bi-monthly newsletter for nurturing support groups, 16535 Ninth Avenue North, Plymouth, Minnesota 55447. Vol. 1, No. 6, July-August, 1980.
2. Thanks to Charlene Pattie for designing and testing the exercise Rejecting Toxic Strokes Internally and Externally.
3. The Extended Stroke Base exercise was inspired by Jerry and Terri White's New Parent "Service Structure" concept.
4. Thanks to Meredith Robinson for designing the Multicolored Daisy Celebration.
5. The suggested format for support group meetings is taken from: *We*. (See above, Note 1)
6. Thanks to Joyce Wong and Renee Fredrickson for designing this assessment instrument.

BIBLIOGRAPHY

Babcock, Dorothy E., and Keepers, Terry D. *Raising Kids O.K.: Transactional Analysis in Human Growth and Development.* New York: Avon Books, 1977.

Berne, Eric. *TA in Psychotherapy.* New York: Grove Press, 1961.

————. *The Structure and Dynamics of Groups.* New York: Grove Press, 1963.

————. *What Do You Say After You Say Hello?* New York: Bantam Books, 1973.

Blos, Peter. *The Adolescent Passage: Developmental Issues.* New York: International Universities Press, 1979.

Bowlby, John. *Child Care and the Growth of Love.* Middlesex, England: Penguin Books, 1953.

Briggs, Dorothy Corkille. *Your Child's Self-Esteem: The Key to Life.* New York: Doubleday, Dolphin Books, 1975.

Capers, Hedges, and Holland, Glen. "Stroke Survival Quotient." *Transactional Analysis Journal* 1, no. 3 (July 1971).

Clarke, Jean Illsley. *Self-Esteem: A Family Affair.* Minneapolis: Winston Press, 1979.

————. "The Terrific Twos." *Child Care Resources.* vol. 4, no. 7 Mound, Minn.: Quality Child Care Press, Inc. (July 1980).

Crary, Elizabeth. *Without Spanking or Spoiling: A Practical Approach to Toddler and Preschool Guidance.* Seattle: Parenting Press, 1979.

Dierks, Sally, "Creative Hassling: Adults and Teenagers Together in a New Way." Unpublished manuscript, 1980.

Dreikurs, Rudolf, and Soltz, Vicki. *Children: The Challenge.* New York: Hawthorn Books, 1964.

Dusay, John. *Egograms.* New York: Harper and Row, 1977.

Duska, Ronald, and Whelan, Mariellen. *Moral Development: A Guide to Piaget and Kohlberg.* New York: Paulist Press, 1975.

Edelwich, Jerry, with Brodsky, Archie. *Burnout: Stages of Disillusionment in the Helping Professions.* New York: Human Sciences Press, 1980.

Ernst, Ken. *Pre-Scription: A TA Look at Child Development.* Millbrae, Calif.: Celestial Arts, 1976.

Faust, Verne. *Five Ways of Parenting: One That Works!* San Diego: Thomas Paine Press, 1980.

Fraiberg, Selma H. *The Magic Years: Understanding and Handling the Problems of Early Childhood.* New York: Scribner, 1968.

Gage, N. L. *Teacher Effectiveness and Teacher Training: The Search for Scientific Basis.* Palo Alto, Calif.: Pacific Books, 1972.

Galinsky, Ellen. *Between Generations: The Six Stages of Parenthood.* New York: Times Books, 1981.

Gordon, Thomas. *Parent Effectiveness Training: The No-Lose Program for Raising Responsible Children.* New York: Peter H. Wyden, Inc., 1970.

Gordon, William J. *Synectics: The Development of Creative Capacity.* New York: The Macmillan Co., 1961.

Gould, Roger. *Transformations: Growth and Change in Adult Life.* New York: Simon and Schuster, 1978.

Greenberg, Selma. *Right from the Start: A Guide to Nonsexist Child Rearing.* Boston: Houghton Mifflin Co., 1978.

Greenburg, Dan, and Jacobs, Marcia. *How to Make Yourself Miserable.* New York: Random House, 1966.

Guthrie, Eileen, and Miller, Warren. *Making Change: A Guide to Effectiveness in Groups.* Minneapolis: Interpersonal Communication Programs, Inc., 1978.

Hall, Edward T. *The Hidden Dimension.* Garden City: Doubleday, Anchor Books, 1969.

Hendricks, Gay, and Wills, Russell. *The Centering Book: Awareness Activities for Children, Parents, and Teachers.* Englewood Cliffs, N.J.: Prentice-Hall, Inc.,1975.

James, Muriel, and Jongeward, Dorothy. *Born to Win: Transactional Analysis with Gestalt Experiments.* Reading, Mass.: Addison-Wesley, 1971.

————. *Transactional Analysis for Moms and Dads: What to Do with Them Now That You've Got Them.* Reading, Mass.: Addison-Wesley, 1974.

Kirschenbaum, Howard, and Simon, Sidney. *Readings in Values Clarifications.* Minneapolis: Winston Press, 1973.

Knowles, Malcolm. *The Modern Practice in Adult Education: Andragogy Versus Pedagogy.* New York: Association Press, 1976.

Lacoursiere, Roy. *The Life Cycle of Groups: Group Developmental Stage Theory.* New York: Human Sciences Press, 1980.

Lankton, Steve. *Practical Magic: A Translation of Basic Neuro-Linguistic Programming into Clinical Psychotherapy.* Cupertino, Calif.: Meta Publications, 1980.

Larson, Roland S., and Larson, Doris E. *Values and Faith: Value-Clarifying Exercises for Family and Church Groups.* Minneapolis: Winston Press, 1976.

LeShan, Eda. *What Makes Me Feel This Way: Growing Up with Human Emotions.* New York: The Macmillan Co., Collier Books, 1974.

Levin, Pamela. *Becoming the Way We Are: A Transactional Guide to Personal Development.* San Francisco, Calif.: Transactional Publications, 1974.

Levin Landheer, Pamela. *The Fuzzy Frequency.* San Francisco, Calif.: Transactional Publications, 1978.

————. "Cycles of Power." Unpublished manuscript, 1980.

Levinson, Daniel J., et al. *The Season of a Man's Life.* New York: Ballantine Books, 1978.

Mager, Robert F. *Goal Analysis.* Belmont, Calif.: Fearon Publishing, 1972.

May, Rollo. *Power and Innocence: A Search for the Sources of Violence.* New York: C. C. Norton, 1972.

————. *The Courage to Create.* New York: Bantam Books, 1976.

Montagu, Ashley. *Touching: The Human Significance of the Skin.* New York: Harper and Row, 1971.

Morris, Desmond. *The Human Zoo.* New York: McGraw-Hill, 1969.

Piaget, Jean. *The Child and Reality.* New York: Penguin Books, Inc., 1976.

Reid, Clyde. *Celebrate the Temporary.* New York: Harper and Row, 1972.

Satir, Virginia. *Peoplemaking.* Palo Alto, Calif.: Science and Behavior Books, 1972.

Satir, Virginia; Stachowiak, James; and Taschman, Harvey A. *Helping Families to Change.* New York: Jason Aronson, Inc., 1976.

Schiff, Jacqui. *Cathexis Reader.* New York: Harper and Row, 1975.

Simon, Sidney; Howe, Leland; and Kirschenbaum, Howard. *Values Clarification: A Handbook of Practical Strategies for Teachers and Students.* New York: Hart Publishing, 1972.

Steiner, Claude. *Scripts People Live: Transactional Analysis of Life Scripts.* New York: Grove Press, 1974.

————. *The Original Warm Fuzzy Tale.* San Francisco, Calif.: Transactional Publications, 1977.

Stinnett, Nick, et al. *Family Strengths: Positive Models for Family Life.* Lincoln, Nebr.: University of Nebraska Press, 1980.

Suchman, Edward. *Evaluative Research: Principles and Practice in Public Service and Social Action Programs.* New York: Russell Sage Foundation, 1976.

Toman, Walter. *Family Constellation: Its Effects on Personality and Social Behavior.* New York: Springer Publishing Co., 1976.

Tough, Allen. *The Adult's Learning Projects: A Fresh Approach to Theory and Practice in Adult Learning.* Toronto: The Ontario Institute for Studies in Education, 1975.

Watzlawick, Paul. *The Language of Change: Elements of Therapeutic Communication.* New York: Basic Books, 1978.

Wells, L. Edward, and Marshall, Gerald. *Self-Esteem: Its Conceptualization and Measurement.* Beverly Hills, Calif.: Sage Publications, 1976.

West, Karen, ed. *Family Day-to-Day Care.* Mound, Minn.: Quality Child Care Press, 1979.

White, Burton L. *The First Three Years of Life.* Englewood Cliffs, N. J.: Prentice-Hall, 1975.

White, Harvey. *Your Family Is Good for You.* New York: Random House, 1978.

Woolams, Stanley; Brown, Michael; and Huige, Kristen. *TA in Brief.* Ann Arbor, Mich.: Huron Valley Institute, 1976.

ACKNOWLEDGMENTS

Thanks to Dick, Marc, Jennifer, and Wade Clarke for being and for helping me.

Thanks to all the people who have participated in the classes, made judgments and suggestions, and celebrated with me. Thanks to Pam Levin Landheer for the use of the material in "Becoming the Way We Are" and for her personal encouragement. Thanks to Wayne Paulson for saying, "Do it." Thanks to Betty Beach, Shirley Bullock, Sally Dierks, Kaara Ettesvold, Claudia Freund, Deane Gradous, Judee Hansord, Sheila Hartmann, Judy Howard, Ann King, Nancy O'Hara, Annette Pattie, Marilyn Sackariason, Karen West, and all the other people who read manuscripts. Thanks to Lexi Cummings, Marita Erickson, Mary LeMar, Gail Nordeman, Harold Nordeman, Jan Schneider, Fran Shultz, Marj Smith, Joan Spindler, and Karen Thiel for testing the model in other parts of the country.

In addition to the people who were mentioned for specific contributions, thanks to all of the facilitators who have made these meetings part of their journey: Bernice Brotherton, Trice Connelly, Ken Daniel, Nancy Delin, Mary Ann Eckenberg, Beth Hallen, Gwen Heinecke, Val Hessburg, Becky Kajander, Val Moore, Jean Peebles, Annetta Shaw, Linda Shipp Martin, Judy Schlichting, John B. Severson, Peggy Shriner, Sandy Sittko, Sue Sorenson, Sandy Stoltz, Sandy Swanson, Dagmar Tisdale, Shann Valentine Bulger, Jean Wagner, Judy Wallshlaeger, and Mary Wood.

Thanks to Marj Smith for reading all the "Letters to Marj."

Thanks to Dee Ready for catching the vision in these meeting plans and shepherding them from the time of early testing to publication. And thanks to Pat Lassonde for her careful and supportive editing.

Thanks for willing and thoughtful typing to Peg Schneider, Wendy Roal, and Carol Eshelman.

Jean Illsley Clarke, author of Self-Esteem: A Family Affair, *founded the child-care workshops, "Mothers, Fathers, and Others Who Care About Children," which grew into the child-and-adult care model described in this manual. Ms. Clarke holds a master's degree in human development from St. Mary's College, Winona, Minnesota. She has been active in adult education for over twenty years and has also worked extensively with children and adolescents. Ms. Clark is married and has three children. She has spent years as the primary caregiver for her children. Ms. Clark is director of J. I. Consultants and has been a consultant for numerous educational institutions, churches, synagogues, human service agencies, and business and community groups.*

Ms. Clark conducts workshops for people who want specific training in facilitating the group learning experiences described in this book. Inquiries about the workshops and other ways to use Self-Esteem: A Family Affair *may be directed to Ms. Clarke, care of Winston Press, 430 Oak Grove, Minneapolis, Minnesota 55403.*

Thoughts on Ending. . . .
I hope you will use this book to help you find ways to grow successfully through your own stages of adult development and to increase your skill in inviting children and other adults to grow and to value themselves and others. I have had an exciting five-year journey developing this model. Thank you for joining me.
        Jean Illsley Clarke